DEEP IN THE HEART
of
SAN ANTONIO

DEEP IN THE HEART
of
SAN ANTONIO

Land and Life in South Texas

CHAR MILLER

TRINITY UNIVERSITY PRESS

San Antonio

Published by Trinity University Press
San Antonio, Texas 78212

Cover design by David Timmons
Book design by BookMatters, Berkeley

⊖ The paper used in this publication meets the minimum
requirements of the American National Standard for Information
Sciences—Permanence of Paper for Printed Library Materials,
ANSI Z39.48-1992.

LIBRARY OF CONGRESS CATALOGING-IN-PUBLICATION DATA

Miller, Char, 1951–
Deep in the heart of San Antonio :
land and life in South Texas / Char Miller.
p.   cm.
Includes index.
ISBN 1-59534-006-8 (hardcover : alk. paper)—
ISBN 1-59534-007-6 (pbk. : alk. paper)
1. San Antonio (Tex.)—History.
2. San Antonio (Tex.)—Environmental conditions.
3. San Antonio (Tex.)—Description and travel.
4. San Antonio (Tex.)—Politics and government.
5. San Antonio Region (Tex.)—History.
6. San Antonio Region (Tex.)—Environmental conditions.
7. San Antonio Region (Tex.)—Description and travel.
8. San Antonio Region (Tex.)—Politics and government.
I. Title.
F394.S11157M55   2004
976.4'351-dc22   2004008914

Printed in the United States of America

06   07   08   /   5   4   3   2

For Gary, Lynne, Emily, & Max

Contents

Preface

Many years ago, while swimming in an outdoor pool in Port Aransas, Texas, my wife and I struck up a conversation with a young girl from The Netherlands who was vacationing at the Gulf Coast beach town with her family. Our chatter, on that warm, sun-kissed day, was as desultory as it was forgettable, except that we still recall her delight when we told her we lived in San Antonio. It was, she exclaimed, her favorite city in Texas. But something about it was odd: "They haven't finished building it yet!"

For all her assumptions about the unchangeable character of the Old World urban centers in which she had grown up, her sense of San Antonio's protean quality was (and is) on the mark. As with other cities in the post–World War Two American West, San Antonio's explosive growth has been tied to the rapid development of the national service economy, the astonishing demographic migration of people from the Northeast and Midwest to the South and Far West, and an immense investment of federal

dollars in the region, funneled through its many military installations, transportation infrastructure, and university or computer
research and development programs.

So profound have these transformations been that Los Angeles, which in the 1950s was the lone western metropolis on the
list of the nation's ten largest cities, has since been joined by five
others—Houston, Phoenix, San Diego, Dallas, and San Antonio.
Add to this list such booming centers as the San Francisco Bay
Area, Salt Lake City, Denver, and Las Vegas, and it becomes clear
why the region dubbed the Sunbelt so captured the public imagination in the go-go 1980s.

The Sunbelt's allure has been reinforced ever since through its
conscious catering to the felt needs of American consumers. "Post-
modern, postindustrial capitalism is about consuming experience,"
historian Hal Rothman has argued in *Neon Metropolis: How Las
Vegas Started the Twenty-first Century*. It is "about creating insa-
tiable desire that must be fulfilled in front of an approving audience." No cities have been more attuned to these self-referential
fantasies than Las Vegas or that other dream manufactory, Los
Angeles. Yet western urban economies and environments in general have done their bit to indulge the whims of those hungry for
the exotic, or what passes for it. And if the elixir of political power
is what excites, then it is also to the West that contemporary
Americans must turn; its swelling electoral clout, ineluctably tied
to its postwar population surge, determines national elections.
John F. Kennedy was the last northern candidate elected president
of the United States, and since 1960 only one occupant of the
White House has come from east of the Mississippi.

That three of the modern presidents have claimed roots in Texas reflects as well just how pivotal the Lone Star State is to the body politic and how quickly it has been transformed by the forces of modernization. Texas officially became urbanized in the mid-1940s, a generation after the rest of the nation had accomplished the transition, but it has since made up for lost ground. In what amounts to a tale of three cities, its contemporary history has revolved around the rapid growth and development of Houston, Dallas, and San Antonio. In 1930, none of the trio topped 300,000 residents, but by the 2000 U.S. Census each had more than one million, and Houston contained nearly two. These cities' ballooning populations have been matched by a startling physical expansion. Liberal annexation codes have allowed them to sprawl in size, so that by the early twenty-first century Dallas was the smallest at 342 square miles, San Antonio was more than 400 and Houston nearly 600. Everything, it seems, is bigger in Texas.

But not equally so. Of the three, San Antonio—the state's largest city until the 1920s—has lagged behind the others in population increase, economic development, and political import. Its citizenry is less well educated, and its middle class is thinner in number and impact—demographic data that help explain why San Antonio remains one of the poorest of America's largest cities, vying with Detroit for that less-than-exalted title. Its poverty is historic and has been linked to its inability and unwillingness to push beyond its dependence on military spending and tourism to fill the communal coffers. That situation has begun to change. Heavy investment in health care and medical services, initiated in the mid-1970s, has nourished a new level of economic activity, resulting in an increase in skill and wage levels. The announcement in early 2003 that giant automaker Toyota would locate a major manufacturing plant on the city's south side may also herald a shift in fortune, allowing San Antonio to finally take advantage of the industrialization that has been the source of its in-state rivals' tremendous growth in wealth, power, and prestige.

Then again, San Antonians might respond, who wants to live in Houston or Dallas? The denizens of this south-central Texas metropolis often disdain the rapacious hustle, snarled traffic, and jangled nerves that seem to define contemporary existence in the truly big cities of the United States. We cheer ourselves up with what we perceive to be our slower pace, beneficent weather, and easy social interactions, our community's quaint charm and exotic feel. And we are applauded in turn by a Lone Star aphorism that asserts, "Texans claim two homes—where they live and San Antonio."

These comforting sentiments allow us to ignore pressing cultural concerns, environmental problems, and social tensions; the city's deficiencies, we tell ourselves, cannot be that bad if outsiders assure us that what we have is so special. And those passing through have been saying just that for a long time. One of these visitors, Frederick Law Olmsted, who as a reporter for the *New York Times* rode into San Antonio in the 1850s, was enchanted with the frontier community's odd and antiquated character; the town, he asserted, like San Francisco, New Orleans, and Savannah, was one of the nation's most unusual cities. One hundred and fifty years later, the community's distinctiveness still beguiles, as its millions of annual visitors would attest.

My fascination with San Antonio was born of ignorance. I

had no idea what to expect when I moved to South Texas in the early 1980s, and I was regularly puzzled by what I encountered. The landscape was utterly unlike that of southern New England where I had grown up, as I discovered when, during my on-campus interview at Trinity University, one of my soon-to-be colleagues in the history department warned me never to drive through a low-water crossing when it was raining. I hadn't a clue what he meant. His caution became gospel, however, the moment I read that a thunderous storm surge had swept away cars trying to race across an oft-dry creek bed.

Bewildering experiences such as this one dovetailed with my emerging interests in environmental studies and urban history. Together they have led me to a series of questions that I have been trying to answer ever since, and that have resulted in *Deep in the Heart of San Antonio*. Why was San Antonio built in a flood basin? How did it become such a tourist destination? Are the city's social relations really so amicable, its political fabric truly multicultural? Why has it been so poor, and for so long?

None of these questions—and their many offshoots—have been easy to answer; often they have led to more conundrums, which I have tried to work through by teasing out the relationship between the community's cultural life, economic activity, and environmental context, and between its politics and society. Fortunately, I have been able to learn from (and lean on) a number of friends who know more about these matters than I do. In particular, I owe a great deal to the insights and arguments of Heywood Sanders and David Johnson, colleagues and collaborators who have taught me much about San Antonio and beyond. Waynne Cox generously shared his encyclopedic knowledge of the history of water in San Antonio. Reporters and editors of the city's two dailies, the *San Antonio Light* (now defunct) and the *San Antonio Express-News*, as well as those at the weekly *San Antonio Current*, have shared their ideas, listened to me ramble on, and published some of my musings. Critical too has been the help I have received from a series of editors at the venerable *Texas Observer*. Lou Dubose and Michael King, and more recently Nate Blakeslee and Barbara Belejack, have schooled me in the state's complex political dynamics; I am grateful too that they have pushed me to lighten my prose, to write in nonacademic ways. Thanks to the University of Pittsburgh Press for permission to reprint a small portion of my chapter, "Where the Buffalo Roamed: Ranching, Agriculture, and the Urban Marketplace," in Char Miller, ed., *On the Border: An Environmental History of San Antonio* (2001). Finally, and more supportive than I have any right to deserve, have been Barbara Ras, director of Trinity University Press, and Sarah Nawrocki, assistant to the director, whose deft editorial comments have made this a much better book.

Deep in the Heart of San Antonio could not have been written, in the end, without the sustaining love and support of my nuclear family. My wife, Judi Lipsett, and our two children, Benjamin and Rebecca, have made life in San Antonio an amazing experience. So have those to whom this volume is dedicated. Gary Kates and Lynne Diamond, and their children Emily and Max, helped turn San Antonio into home. Although they have now moved on to new cities and different lives, our affective bonds are as thickly intertwined as the gnarled live oaks that arch over the street on which we lived.

A BIRD'S-EYE VIEW

Best-Laid Plans

San Antonio, the nation's ninth largest city, loves to party. So you would think if your only source of information were the snappy four-color brochures and quick-cut television advertisements that the local Convention and Visitors Bureau generates. These glitzy promotional materials stress the city's festive air, capturing its almost monthly whirl of pageants and parades—from the late-winter Stock Show and Rodeo to April's fortnight-long Fiesta celebrations; from the Folklife Festival in the heat of the summer to the cooler December reenactment of *Las Posadas*, Joseph and Mary's fruitless search for a room in Bethlehem, which files along the fabled Riverwalk. The biblical story line is all too contemporary, as any tourist can attest, for the hotels that crowd the narrow stream's banks are usually packed. But while the Visitors Bureau might not acknowledge that bit of inconvenience in its press releases (though surely its sales objective is a host of glowing No Vacancy signs), it's not shy about promoting San Antonio as a town of fun and frolic.

At the core of this image is the community's Spanish past and Hispanic present. The European explorers pushed north from Mexico and through what is now called south-central Texas in the late seventeenth century: the first local mission, San Antonio de Valero—later called the Alamo—was established in the 1690s, and the city itself was officially platted in 1730. That heritage has endured in demography and lore. Today the city's Hispanic majority (more than 55 percent of the total urban population) is a powerful force in politics and government, education, and commerce, as reflected in the May 2001 election of former councilman Ed Garza as mayor. Garza, the second Hispanic to lead the city in the modern era, followed in the footsteps of his role model, Henry Cisneros. But these elements of civic connection and contribution are not what the public relations agents hype. Their focus is on the brightly hued dresses that flare as women dance the traditional steps of Mexican folkloric ballet on sultry summer eves, their heels drumming on the wooden stage of the Arneson River Theater, and on the strolling mariachi bands, whose wailing, romantic tunes fill the air. Steeped in an exotic heritage, San Antonio is a place apart.

Much of this hard sell is overdone; in more than two decades in San Antonio, I have seen more mariachis in print than in the flesh. Yet the city's Spanish legacy endures, and it surfaces in surprising ways, even in events that appear to bear no trace of the town's colorful history.

"First Friday Art Walk" is the moniker for the monthly block party in San Antonio's Southtown, a recently articulated area that lies, as the name suggests, south of downtown. A mile or so from

Alamo Plaza, site of the infamous 1836 battle, the neighborhood, which consists of mostly nineteenth-century housing and commercial nodes, has as its spine the meandering Alamo Street. The party's name seems innocuous enough, but its last word is of first importance. It may be a modest claim, but what makes this local celebration work is that its participants are on foot, strolling up and down Alamo, crowding into its many galleries and shops, restaurants, and bars. As the sun fades, this traffic intensifies. A sea of heads bobs along between the northern pole, anchored by the trendy restaurant Rosario's, and the southern pole, framed by Blue Star Art Space, which is a former warehouse converted into studios, a microbrewery, and a restaurant. The two-hour journey reminded me just how much the construction of face-to-face communities depends on the ability to *see* others' faces. True, some of the eyes I gazed upon were a bit less focused than others, but whatever their inebriated state, my fellow travelers were reenacting what was once a daily ritual in eighteenth- and nineteenth-century San Antonio—people-watching along *las calles* of the city.

Why does that matter? Because in postmillennial San Antonio, which is utterly dependent on the automobile and the infinite mobility its four wheels seem to provide, we daily flee the very human set of interactions that once made this community so livable. The only people who are immersed in the walker's experience, ironically enough, are our millions of visitors; their languid movements up and down the Riverwalk—to shop, eat, and talk— evoke what once was daily fare on the city's streets and many plazas. But there is hope for the locals: the car has not completely run riot, or so a resurgent Southtown suggests. The area's vitality implies that it would do us a world of good, from time to time, to hop out of the four-cylinder machine and take a quiet stroll into the past.

No one loved the passing parade more than Spanish urban planners. Everywhere they laid down a spatial structure that compelled the citizens of New Spain to revolve around a civic center, timing their movements to the comings and goings of their neighbors as they worked, played, and prayed. That was the stated ambition for the villa of San Fernando de Béxar, when in 1730 the Viceroy of Mexico issued the formal order designing this new colonial settlement, soon to become home to sixteen families from the Canary Islands. Drawing on the prescribed urban form denoted in the Law of the Indes (1583), *Plano de la población* began with the *Yglesia*, the city's eighteenth-century cathedral.

Sited to the west of the San Antonio River, and thus on the opposite side of the watercourse from the mission San Antonio de Valero (the Alamo), the rough-hewn limestone edifice served as the pivot around which the rest of the civilian community would revolve. From what was planned to be its western-facing front door, the streets and plaza were marked off, followed by sur-rounding public buildings and individual housing, all locked in a grid that marched proportionately westward, forming "a cross with the church as a center." This circulatory pattern stimulated a vibrant street life, especially in the plaza. The joyful celebrants of the annual feasts of Our Lady of Guadalupe and San Fernando Rey de España crowded into its open-aired space; the noise of merchants and shoppers haggling over prices rose amid the dust;

and local gossip, like the fragrant scent of grilled meat that permeated the air, wafted through the plaza. For eighteenth-century San Antonians, this urban landscape was the communal heart.

Yet no sooner had the first civilians arrived from the Canary Islands in early March 1731 than Captain Juan Pérez de Almazán recognized a serious flaw in the city's original layout. "The land to the west of the presidio, the location of the said villa, has no facilities for irrigation," he wrote, and the settlers had no time to rectify the situation, as "the present season is the time of the year for preparing the ground for planting corn." Because a crop failure would have doomed the new community, and in response to the dominant position of the mission, which claimed the heights on the eastern bank of the river, Almazán spun the 1730 map on its axis, so that the church's front door now faced east (making its orientation quite unusual in New Spain). This reorientation pushed the villa into land situated between San Pedro Creek and the Big Bend of the San Antonio River, which in time would be the space incorporated into the Riverwalk. Almazán's alteration was not the last time a planner's dream collapsed under the weight of reality.

The revised model generated new dilemmas. In locating the villa west of the river, Almazán unwittingly created social tension between the new center of population and the smaller settlement that had clustered around the mission. This strain would increase in the 1840s following the Mexican-American War as Alamo Plaza became the locus of Euro-American commerce in a predominately Hispanic town. Almazán's decision also led to some disastrous environmental consequences. The search for irrigable land put the farming community smack in the middle of a flood plain. As a late-eighteenth-century visitor complained, "the streets are . . . filled with mud the minute it rains."

Heavy storms brought greater danger. In July 1819, surging waters crashed into the village. From "the proximity of the walls of the San Valero Mission to San Pedro Creek, which crosses behind the city on the West, it was all one river," wrote a sorrowful Gov. Antonio Martínez. Residents and *jacales* (the local mud-and-wattle housing) were sucked into the "irresistible current"; it was "impossible to give immediate aid to the miserable souls who struggled against death," the governor mourned, "because no one could do anything except to look out for himself." This disaster would repeat itself over the course of the city's history, most spectacularly in the devastating floods of 1921, in which more than fifty people were killed; in 1998, in which more than a dozen lost their lives; and in July 2002, when property losses amounted to tens of millions of dollars.

Yet in 1819, even a century-level flood could not alter the physical shape or character of this walking city, and neither could the shifting tides of politics. San Antonio grew slowly during its first 150 years, watching the Spanish, Mexicans, and early Americans come and go. In 1803, it contained an estimated 2,500 people, and in 1870 only 12,000. It absorbed newcomers by expanding the original design, a Spanish motif wherein residential areas and commercial activity fronted open space. This was as true for the new Anglo and German sections of town (largely to river's east and north) as it was for older Hispanic neighborhoods (almost exclusively west of the river). As an 1873 bird's-eye view of the now

American city reveals, contemporary development encircled Washington and Franklin Squares on the west side and Madison and Travis Squares on the east.

Almazán's urban design could not withstand the arrival of the railroad, however. On February 16, 1877, the Galveston, Harrisburg, and San Antonio Railroad blew into town, its screeching whistle heralding a new urban order. Within twelve months, mule-drawn trolley cars began hauling passengers between the east side GHSA railroad station, downtown offices and shops, and new, more distant neighborhoods. By the early 1880s, another line, the International and Great Northern, laid down its tracks on the city's west side, stimulating another round of streetcar development. San Antonio's population grew quickly, rising to more than 37,000 residents in 1890. This boom established a new white majority, many of whom moved to suburbs built along streetcar lines that rose up the low hills to the north of San Pedro Park and to the east of downtown; they commuted back into town to work in the businesses, stores, and shops that lined the major east-west streets of Houston, Commerce, and Market. Giving rise to an ever sharper distinction between work and home, and carrying a population that had enough disposable income to make the transit between the two, the new transportation grid also intensified social prejudice and class distinctions. In a walking city, the rich and poor—whatever they thought of the situation— were compelled to live in close quarters; that proximity was no longer necessary in the Age of the Iron Horse, and the physical gap and psychological distance between the haves and have-nots widened.

By the late nineteenth century, the disappearance of the once open plazas signaled that shared civic space was fast becoming a thing of the past. City hall was dropped into the center of Plaza de las Armas (Military Plaza), which extended from the rear of San Fernando Cathedral and obliterated the cathedral's former role as a center of commercial exchange and pedestrian interchange on the western edge of downtown. Less disrupted was Main Plaza, which lay to the cathedral's immediate east and was the site of the communal marketplace; a portion of its southern flank, however, was sliced off when Market Street was widened for streetcar and vehicular traffic. Even venerated Alamo Plaza was subjected to reconstruction; Crockett Street was cut through it to enhance access to and movement of the increasing tourist trade through the former mission's grounds. To the north, newer squares such as Crockett and Madison would suffer the same fate; when merchants, residents, and planners advocated that streets bisect the squares to boost property values and facilitate traffic flow, the city responded favorably, action that it replicated with other open space well into the 1950s.

As politicians and developers reconfigured the community's original urban form, local observers began to rewrite its social relations. Their words helped legitimize the widening economic gulf between its residents and shifts in the ethnic character of the city's population. By the late nineteenth century, whites dominated in numbers and wealth; Hispanics were a large minority, but along with the tiny black population they were among the city's poorest residents.

Flip though any tourist guide from the late nineteenth and

early twentieth centuries and it is clear that visitors to San Antonio were clued into this growing divide in demography and power: the requisite and patronizing narrative tour of the west side "Mexican Quarter" was inevitably filled with the stock figures of racialist fiction. Somnolent males, their eyes shaded by wide-brimmed hats, loitered in doorways; winsome and barefoot children begged in the streets. It wasn't just the "savory odors of mysterious Mexican viands" that lured locals and tourists alike to Military Plaza, Frank Bushick winked in *Glamorous Days* (1934); the famed Chili Queens' "rich olive skin and the languorous grace and bewitching black eyes" had a smoldering appeal. In the hands of their literary creators, these romanticized types made exotic (and thereby denied) the real-life poverty in which many of their Hispanic subjects were entrenched.

This studied denial was made concrete in the aftermath of the deadly flood of 1921. Its swift waters tore through the city's infrastructure, savaged the west side barrios, and killed more than fifty people, making it the city's deadliest flood. In response, the citizenry voted to float a bond to construct Olmos Dam and to underwrite drainage work along the dangerous west side creeks. But the gross discrepancies in public funding—several million dollars for the dam, a couple thousand for creek brush clearing—reveal how much more valuable the commercial core was perceived to be than the largely Hispanic west side.

The automobile only made matters worse. Beyond the means of all but the middle and upper classes, the early automobiles stimulated the development of high-end suburbs sited just outside the city limits. In the early 1920s, the metropolitan population climbed to just over 161,000, and its economy expanded beyond its original agricultural and ranching base to include military spending (the city was then home to three major army bases), banking, some oil refining, and an emerging tourist trade. A series of new subdivisions to house the rich were built. The Woodlawn neighborhood northwest of downtown was constructed at the same time as Terrell Hills and Olmos Park, lying to its north and east; in between the latter two communities was an older streetcar suburb, Alamo Heights, which also absorbed a new wave of car-happy residents. The moneyed were pulling up and out of town, often taking their tax dollars with them into freshly incorporated communities, making ever more tenuous the links between the rich and poor. The growing physical distance between the classes had political consequences: the elite of this generation disenfran-chised itself, calculating that it could continue to profit from the urban economy without shouldering its share of responsibility for the costs of governance.

That calculation would be harder to maintain as the city started to flex its annexation muscles in the 1940s. But even as it pursued those fleeing its taxation powers, it funneled local, state, and federal monies into expressway construction that sped up sprawl; city zoning ordinances and federal low-cost mortgages added further encouragement to those of the city's now 500,000 who could get out *to* get out. This complicated process was espe-cially manifest during the reign of the Good Government League (GGL), a north side–dominated political machine that gained power in the early 1950s and governed for the next twenty years. Two examples: in locating a new medical center on land adjacent

to the new intersection of Interstate 10 and Loop 410, approximately fifteen miles from downtown, and in platting the University of Texas at San Antonio campus another five miles out IH-10,
it flung public assets into undeveloped land, encouraging increased dispersal. This produced the expected political gains: the
strategy lined the pockets of developers who were major supporters of GGL policies. They in turn created new subdivisions that
were annexed, and from which the GGL drew electoral support.

Although in time the GGL would fall, its developmental
strategies have continued apace. Since the 1970s, as the population
swelled from 700,000 to nearly a million, many found shelter in a
new landscape, known locally as Loopland—the land arcing
between Loops 410 and 1604, which was once home to cattle
grazing amid thickets of oak and juniper. The area has attracted so
much investment that it has become the new, if diffused, downtown. Its undifferentiated mass of tract housing, traditional malls,
and big-box strip centers are perfect markers of the automotive
era. And so, like other parts of the country, the variegated terrain
here has been flattened into parking lots and the city's freeways have created a monotonous built landscape that looks like
Anywhere USA. The monotony is also economic: national retail
chains dominate commercial activity at the expense of San
Antonio–owned businesses. Wheels, not feet, define this modern
cityscape.

There seems to be no end to this revolutionary process. Ex-
urban migration, which began in the 1920s, now spills into the
northern counties of Medina, Kendall, and Comal, as well as
to Wilson and Atascosa Counties to the south. Predictably, this

boom has spawned social problems reminiscent of the dilemmas that those who are moving out are desperate to avoid—more roads, more cars, higher crime, more pollution, greater angst.

Just as predictably, San Antonio has filed extraterritorial jurisdiction claims on segments of the adjacent counties to corral this movement. It is no surprise that these claims are as deeply resented as they are hotly contested. Yet the dispute may be a blessing in disguise, for if successfully walled off from leapfrogging ever outward, San Antonio might be forced to acknowledge the central tension embedded in its ballooning size: how to build a livable community for the roughly 1.5 million residents living within its more than 460 square miles.

Part of the solution lies in putting the brakes on the land rush, particularly to the city's north and west. This halt would have an immediate benefit—preserving imperiled regional water supplies. Beneath the northern tree-studded hills so beloved by developers and homeowners lies the recharge zone for the Edwards Aquifer, essentially the sole source of the city's water (and for many neighboring populations stretching ninety miles west to Uvalde and seventy miles north to Austin). Because urban sprawl compromises the aquifer's capacity to replenish itself and generates pollution—due to parking-lot runoff, lawn fertilizers, and oil spills—grassroots organizations since the 1970s have campaigned hard to counter these threats. Alas, legal challenges to shopping centers and subdivisions, Endangered Species Act–based lawsuits to force the city to locate additional sources of potable water, and a tree preservation ordinance to shape the character of new construction have had only a modest impact. But these tactics have

raised the community's consciousness about the pressures building on the urban fringe. The fight for clean water and green space
is a valiant attempt to release that stress before it tears us apart.

Ditto for efforts to rebuild the central core. As the nascent
drive to redevelop Southtown indicates, concerted actions to re-
vitalize inner-city housing stock and related commercial enterprises offer us a way out of two dilemmas. By salvaging older
neighborhoods—at once making them affordable, amenable, and
viable—we can offer alternative living environments to those who
might otherwise join and reinforce the outward surge. Redi-
recting population away from the booming edge and reinvesting
in the kind of mixed-use, socially integrated, and pedestrian-
friendly streetscapes the Spanish first platted in this city more
than 270 years ago will also help eradicate some of the racial inequalities and economic disparities built into automotive suburbs.
The well-heeled and the less fortunate may never see eye to eye,
but they will have a harder time ignoring, disdaining, or dismiss-
ing each other if they have to look one another *in* the eye. To build
a landscape that requires more physical contact and more face
time, San Antonians had best look to their past. History matters.

The benefits of the backward glance are already visible. In
areas as diverse as Monticello Park, Monte Vista, King William,
Lavaca, and Dignowity Hill, neighborhood activists and historic
preservationists have long demonstrated that restoration of older
homes and in-fill of empty lots can pay off in ways that are aesthetic, economic, and psychological. Similar gains may be realized
on the city's historic black east side, with the revitalization of the
Carver Community Cultural Center complex (to which NBA

All-Star David Robinson of the San Antonio Spurs has donated more than $9 million to launch a high-quality private school for low-income children) and the rehab of the nearby cavernous, abandoned Friedrich Air Conditioning Co. factory, which is slated for offices and shops. Such benefits are even being realized in the once toxic landscape on Cherry Street, to the south and east of downtown. Following revelations of dangerous pollutants leaching into the soil from a former ironworks, torn down in advance of the construction of the Alamodome, the surrounding area was flattened. And then rebuilt. City agencies, in conjunction with the Parade of Homes and a group of committed residents, have invested a great deal of money, time, and labor to reclaim this bulldozed working-class neighborhood. The historic echoes in the new homes' architecture and the planting of indigenous flora suggest how we can turn a brownfield into greensward.

The ambition to recreate human-scale environments and intimate walking districts may lack the pizzazz of a slick video promoting the fab time awaiting those who visit San Antonio, but it offers something a good deal more significant. If replicated citywide, such recreations would enable us to rebuild—or, where possible, build from scratch—neighborhoods that offer a scintillating blend of housing styles and sizes and that can cut across class lines, provide an array of consumer activities, and be sources of decent work opportunities. As these develop, one block at a time, they would also help us stitch back together our disparate, often far-flung, neighborhoods into an urban whole.

That imagined reality has already begun to emerge in the Southtown area, and it caught the eye of some Trinity University first-year students who were participating in a weeklong preorientation program centered at the nearby Mennonite church. By day, they worked in soup kitchens or built entry ramps for elderly who were disabled or simply had trouble navigating stairways; by night, they met with faculty, city officials, and nonprofit social service providers to learn more about the city they would call home for the next four years. When I asked a group of these students, who came from all over the country, what struck them about the neighborhood, a number piped up that the architecture, dating back to the nineteenth century, was quite different from the suburban uniformity they were used to. Others mentioned that the very fact that they walked to and from their day's activities was unusual, allowing them to see what they might have missed had they driven through. One young woman, who grew up in a tightly segregated middling Texas city, was puzzled by what she had never seen in her hometown: families congregating on their porches, people-filled sidewalks, and young men talking to (and occasionally whistling at) the students as they moved past. Another framed the interactive bustle in terms of the range and social status of the cars—from late-model Jaguars to hopped-up low-riders to kid-packed minivans—that cruised down the streets. And several others noted that a single block might contain houses big and small, rehabbed and falling down—a jumble that was reflected in local demographics: Latinos, Anglos, and blacks living side by side. "It doesn't seem to matter who you are down here" was one student's excited conclusion. Which is another way of saying that we need more, and more fully realized, Southtowns. Sounds like a plan.

Torch Song

A massive, eye-popping piece of public sculpture was raised in downtown San Antonio in mid-2002, creating a moment of considerable controversy. Ordinary citizens, commentators in the arts and the media, and politicians and radio deejays battled over the size, bold color, artistic merit, and cultural significance of *La Antorcha de la Amistad* (Torch of Friendship), a sixty-five-foot, forty-five-ton structure designed by the Mexican sculptor Sebastián. The fight is ironic, for Sebastián indicated that his work was designed to celebrate the harmonious relationship between Mexico and the United States. Yet even the abstract sculpture's pacific intent sparked discord.

To evoke binational harmony, Sebastián constructed a pair of red steel columns that, although separated by twenty feet at ground level, bend and fold together as they rise skyward. At the circular apex—a piece that by itself weighs 15,000 pounds—a single shaft of light rises into the night sky. The striking four-story structure was formally dedicated in late June 2002.

Its dedication did not slow the debate. That was because the Torch's siting, smack in the middle of the busy downtown confluence of Commerce, Alamo, and Losoya Streets, was as provocative as waving a red flag at a bull. Its central location fed into San Antonio's history of pillorying contemporary artwork. In the past, a roused citizenry has vented its sharp displeasure in the press, civic forums, and on right-wing radio talk shows. Often grumpily dismissive of abstract art, this small army of noisy critics has been especially perturbed when tax dollars are doled out to its creators. In the early 1990s, their animosity was so fierce that it fueled some politicians' careers while sending others down in flames. That the Torch would get torched was predictable.

Opposition this time was muted, however, because the massive sculpture was a $650,000 gift from the Mexican government and the Asociación de Empresarios Mexicanos, an organization of Mexican business leaders who live or work in San Antonio. But the fact that people could not complain about the cost to local taxpayers did not stop them from voicing their disagreements. Some gawkers were turned off by the Torch's enchilada-red color scheme. The San Antonio Conservation Society, a powerful historic preservation lobby, feared that the sculpture's modernistic flair clashed with downtown's nineteenth-century ambience. Others worried that the dazzling project would be a dangerous distraction for drivers as they entered and revolved around the traffic circle in which it had been placed. "For those of us who drive by it regularly," an exasperated Michael Mehl declared in the locally published *Voices of Art* magazine, "its most salient feature is how much it obstructs the view of traffic, making an informed left turn from any direction rather difficult." Then there were questions of social justice: "A $650,000 'symbol' when people are going hungry?" queried a correspondent to the *San Antonio Express-News*. "Thumbs down on both sides of the border."

Innumerable on-camera interviews inevitably focused on perplexed passersby unschooled in the nuances of modern art. Asked what he thought of the abstract monument, one man spoke for many: "I don't get it." This general confusion, a *raspa* vendor asserted, was reflective of the city's conservative tastes. "I know it's a tribute," Nhora Prieto told a reporter, "but for San Antonio, hmmm, I don't know." Critic Mehl, for whom modernism was not an unfamiliar concept, made his disdain known when he affected to "leave all value judgments—whether the piece is derivative or trite—for future scholars and art historians to hash out."

This is hardly the first time Sebastián, who has built towering abstract structures in many of the world's great cities, has been the target of criticism. A particular stunning example of his provocative monumentalism is *Cabeza de caballo*, located at the intersection of Avenida Juárez and Paseo de la Reforma in Mexico City. The sculpture's installation in 1992 generated outrage. People fulminated about its size (ninety-two feet), color (bright yellow), and abstract expression, bringing it far greater renown than it might otherwise have enjoyed. The San Antonio Chamber of Commerce and the local tourist bureau can but hope the same will be true of *La Antorcha de Amistad*.

That the Torch may soon become a tourist attraction raises another set of questions about its impact and import. Although beautifully realized, the sculpture miscasts the past. Its clean, slick, fluid lines belie the messy relations between Mexico and the United States. The border between the two countries seems as embattled now as when it was forcibly laid down in the nineteenth century. As a consequence of the Mexican-American War, in which a vast chunk of Mexico disappeared into the American union, boundary skirmishes disrupted diplomatic ties for decades. They do not seem any more sanguine today, as reflected in the sharpening debate over the distribution of the Rio Grande's streamflow, ongoing battles over Mexican migration to and the immigrant's status in the United States, American labor unions' furious attempts to halt Mexican truckers from rolling down the nation's interstate highway system (itself an aftershock of the controversial NAFTA treaty), and the charges and countercharges over cross-border drug trafficking.

These durable disputes are also bound up with persistent cultural ties, from architecture to language to religion, a connectivity that disrupts the standard narrative of the history of the United States. From childhood, we are taught that a straight line linked early-seventeenth-century New England Puritans to mid-nineteenth-century Texas buckaroos and California forty-niners; from sea to shining sea, westward the course of empire. That line was anything but straight, and its presumed east-west movement was yet another form of cultural imperialism. History in the southwestern United States, as timed by the Spanish arrival, moved north-south, and that pulse has remained central to San Antonio's understanding of itself, as enacted in the street vernacular, educational missions, commercial exchanges, and social ties. These orientations, ephemeral and enduring, transcend sculptural sentiments of friendship.

Perhaps it was too much to ask that the Torch convey the full dynamism of U.S.-Mexico interactions, but in ignoring complexity Sebastián has given us a past too abstracted from its thickly tangled roots. With that, he left himself vulnerable to Mehl's racialist snarl that the statue is "the ultimate wet-dream come true, for all of Santa Ana's self-appointed descendants: they have finally taken back the Alamo."

Grant the artist this triumph, however modest: his controversial sculpture has forced many San Antonians to wrestle with the purpose of public art. Count me among them, for I was dubious of its evocative power—that is, until I set eyes on it one humid summer's eve. It rattled my conceit when, after circling it from afar, I crossed the empty street to walk within its towering presence. Like a Rorschach test, *La Antorcha de Amistad* forced to mind my stunning failure to learn Spanish despite living in this bilingual city for more than two decades, a tongue-tied embarrassment deftly captured in Sebastián's blush-red structure of twisted steel.

Concrete Ends

On a late-night run from the San Antonio airport to my home, I peered out of the taxi as it zipped past the ghostly remains of the Alamo Cement company—a gutted factory and five tall smokestacks, the corporate name still emblazoned on them. My loquacious cabbie began laughing. "Listen," he said. "You're not going to believe this. Last month I was carrying a group of Japanese scientists downtown for a convention. When they saw those stacks they asked me to stop so they could take some photographs." He recounted how he pulled to the side of busy McAllister Freeway and watched as the scientists snapped away. "When they piled back in," he said, "they politely thanked me for showing them the Alamo." He leaned back and grinned. "Tourists."

He was right: I didn't really believe his tall tale about cross-cultural confusions, but then I don't think I was supposed to. Besides, his was not the best gag about this abandoned infrastructure and its dusty environs. That distinction surely belonged to the developers who announced with great flourish in 1995 that they planned to turn the vast cement works into an upscale 500,000-square-foot shopping mall.

It's not that I doubted their intentions. On the contrary, this proposed project was the last stage of a massive conversion of the sprawling 450-acre site the cement plant once occupied. Beginning in the mid-1980s, a series of developments sprouted up: first a retail strip mall with an architecture more imposing than the shops it contains and then "prestige garden homes," precariously perched on the edge of the abandoned quarry, which itself was later domesticated. Today a carpet of green grass lines its floor and weaves around an artificial lake, an odd contrast to the rough-cut limestone walls. Odder still is that this is home to an eighteen-hole golf course. These amenities come with others designed to soothe one's soul. The glittering and commodious Alamo Heights United Methodist Church, so large that it has been dubbed the Methodome, lies cheek-by-jowl with swank senior housing.

We can shop until we drop, too. The list of tenants in the touted mall reads like a Who's Who of haute retailing, ranging from Borders Books and Music and Whole Foods Market to Starbucks Coffee and Restoration Hardware. Those for whom ice cream must be a high butterfat experience can find it at Amy's Ice Cream. All this and more (restaurants, a multiplex movie theater, and a health club) have been encased in the glass-walled cavernous "clinker" shed, where a rattling rush of rock aggregate once poured to form an endless stream of cement. When it was completed in the late fall of 1997, the Alamo Quarry Market Shopping Center (a.k.a. the Quarry) offered the final and fullest sign that this former zone of heavy industry had been transformed into a bourgeois dreamscape of consumption.

Here is where the gag comes in, especially if you like your humor dark: beneath this manufactured landscape of plenty are buried the vestiges of a vibrant working-class neighborhood called Cementville. Founded in 1914 shortly after the plant opened, Cementville became home to generations of workers and their families. Its almost exclusively Hispanic population paid $15 to $20 a month to rent three-room, company-owned houses located on streets named Ortiz, Ponce, Robles, or Peña, each a short walk from the St. Anthony of Padua parish, where the residents worshiped. They belonged to the Union Fraternal Mexicana, which through song and poetry sought to perpetuate Mexican culture. Their children were educated at the on-site Bluebonnet School (rather than attending the Anglo-dominated elementary school in nearby Alamo Heights), and Cinco de Mayo and Diez y Seis de Septiembre were plant holidays. Hard as their life and labor was, it is easy to understand why the quarry workers and their families wistfully recall splashing in the company-built Olympic-size swimming pool or sharing the desertlike terrain with armadillos and roadrunners, foxes and deer. All this gave shape to what one worker remembered as Cementville's "profound sense of community."

That sensibility was obliterated with the plant's closing and thoroughly interred with the completion of the Quarry Market. So it was with the site's natural environment, in a reconfiguration so thorough that what area outsiders once denigrated as "the ghetto of Alamo Heights" has become the exclusive suburb's crowning glory, bearing an appropriately elevated moniker: Lincoln Heights.

This transition reflected an upward turn in San Antonio's economic fortunes, increasingly tied to high-end merchandising keyed to its burgeoning upper middle class. The reason for this shift toward consumption is revealed in U.S. Department of Commerce data about the city's average income. In 1985, it stood at $13,500, by 1996 it had risen to more than $18,000, and by 2002 it had climbed into the low twenties—a steady rise largely attributable to the importation of work and managerial salaries. The relocation of Southwestern Bell's national headquarters to the city and the rapid expansion of the medical center and associated white-collar occupations boosted the averages. The well-heeled consumers who earn these salaries are the market that the Quarry was designed to attract.

The shopping mall was not constructed to lure the less well shod. The plight of this group, however, has only intensified. What the Commerce Department's income figures do not indicate is the corresponding and irretrievable loss of blue-collar employment. Since the late 1970s, jobs in San Antonio's slaughterhouses and clothing industry, as well as in its few foundries and factories, have all but evaporated. This, when coupled with the steady downsizing in civilian employment at the city's many military installations, has continued to diminish the opportunities for San Antonio's largely Hispanic working class to achieve middleclass standing. Low-wage service jobs are no substitute for higher-skilled and better-paid industrial labor.

These dwindling economic options have impaired our ability to acknowledge Cementville's past and the substantial contributions its workers made to the city's development and its local economy. In time we will see those preserved smokestacks rising above the Alamo Quarry Market and, like the apocryphal Japanese tourists, assume they stand for something other than what they were. And when that happens, it will signal that we have fully lost touch with a history we have already begun to forget.

Shell Game

I don't much like the common grackle. Sure, it has a lyrical Latin handle, *Quiscalus quiscula,* and the male's plumage is a sharp-looking, iridescent purplish black, but those qualities simply mask the fact that this bird is a loudmouthed boor.

Its call—a grating, ascending squeak—is bad enough played solo; when grackles roost with their cohorts in a tree, the cacophony is unnerving. For some reason the birds especially like San Antonio's Riverwalk, and they congregate along its banks in such large numbers that park rangers have fired starter's pistols to make them take flight. They should have used live ammunition.

Then again, had they all been gunned down, they would not have taught me the value of a cracked nut. Early one windswept, cold December morning, I tracked a grackle as it swooped to the ground, deftly grasped a pecan in its beak, and soared to a nearby mesquite. It paused, then took off, threading its way between a magnolia and a live oak bent in the stiff breeze. As it flew over the street, it dropped its cargo just moments before a car approached.

The Volvo station wagon failed to do its business—or rather the task I imagined the grackle had in mind for it—but I took the hint: I brought my heel down on the pecan, and pivoted, before sauntering up the road toward the sunrise.

It did not dawn on me until later what I had witnessed. But I began to sense its import as I looped around our pecan-studded neighborhood. Everywhere that morning I spied Inca and mourning doves—and grackles, too—pecking away at ground nut fragments littering the streets. They weren't the only ones to take advantage of the free meal. Nutmeg, our aging golden retriever, who has a sharp nose for pecans, was lapping up the morning's spread. People were grazing, too, slowly moving along the curbs and beneath the leafless trees, bending down to scoop up handfuls of the smooth, brown casing; their pockets, like a squirrel's cheeks, were bulging.

The previous evening's norther, a blustery cold front, had hurled down this bounty, providing a rich diet for all, a vivid reflection of the complex ties binding streetscape and landscape, flora and fauna, humanity and nature. As any grackle might testify, the pecan is integral to the identity of South Texas.

That has long been true. Some of the first words recorded about the region spoke of the nut's centrality in human affairs. Cabeza de Vaca, who wandered as a captive throughout the southern portions of the state between 1528 and 1536, spoke of the numerous groves he encountered along the area's many rivers. It was to the Guadalupe, which Cabeza called the "river of nuts," that his captors annually migrated to harvest the nutritious meat. Their food preparation was simple—the Indians ground up the nuts "with a kind of small grain"—but the result must have satisfied: "This is the subsistence of the people two months in the year without any other thing," Cabeza wrote.

The seasonal diet of later Spanish colonizers may have been a touch more varied, but they too delighted in breaking open the nut's thin brown shell. As they devoured its contents, they found, as did Father Espinosa in 1709, that these Texas nuts were "more tasty and palatable than those of Castile." In this claim lay a message: the missionaries were becoming quite comfortable in the New World, this New Spain. And that spelled bad news for the indigenous residents. Many were struck down by imported diseases or converted (often forcibly) to a new religion and absorbed into a more settled agricultural economy. Their loss was the Spaniards' gain. The winnowing away of the Payaya and Tonkawa, the Semomam, Saracuam, and Anxau, and other bands of hunter-gatherers opened the way for astute colonials to head for the woods and market the autumn pecan harvest. They gathered well. In 1791, for example, Antonio Baca left San Antonio for nearby provinces to sell sixteen mules loaded down with pecans. So brisk was the trade, and so closely identified with this northern frontier outpost, that pecans were dubbed "San Antonio nuts."

That connection remained tight even as the small, preindustrial village slowly evolved in the mid-nineteenth century into a bustling American city. European and American travelers to the region made note of the substantial trade in pecans. One who regularly trafficked in them was Reading Black, a founder of Uvalde, ninety miles west. With his home and store sited directly beside the busy road between San Antonio and more western settlements, Black had his fingers in a lot of pies. On December 20, 1854, a wagon rolled in from San Antonio and he "bought a load of pecans for $1.12½ per bush[el]." Within hours he had traded some of this commodity with a nearby Tonkawan settlement and purchased shirts from a passing trader. For him and many others, pecans were just another form of exchange.

They became some people's daily bread, especially during the grim years immediately following the Civil War. An 1871 report noted that, but "for the industry of nut gathering, the people of some localities must have starved for lack of remunerative labor. Hundreds of both white and colored people go out with horses and wagons to gather these nuts." In hard times, the newest humans in Texas reenacted an ancient ritual.

But reliance on native habits and indigenous habitats would disappear by the end of the nineteenth century, when the production of and commerce in pecans became more formal and substantial. In 1880, Mexican American teamsters hauled an estimated 1.25 million pounds into San Antonio, from which they were shipped by rail to pecan fanciers across the nation. By 1919, Bexar County alone produced more than 370,000 pounds of pecans, running a close second to Llano County's productivity in a state that led the nation in pecan harvesting. These numbers suggest that the indigenous tree had come under sustained cultivation, a mark of the pacification of the South Texas landscape. That transformation could not have come too quickly, bemoaned George Tyng, a Victoria grower: "No more costly mistakes have I made than in trying to follow nature in raising pecans. Every agri-cultural success has been achieved by overcoming nature's efforts to defeat it."

The triumph Tyng desired was manifest in contemporary experiments in seedling orchards, new techniques in pruning and grafting, and advances in asexual propagation. These increased the productive capacity of and capital investment in the new groves, which, by the end of the nineteenth century, triggered a speculative frenzy. In the classic pattern of boom-bust cycles that periodically rocked the American economy, investors anted up in the "pecan game," not, an observer decried, for "the profits they anticipated out of this crop, but through the money they could make selling the orchards." Get-rich schemes abounded and for-tunes were made as quickly as they were lost, all of which testified that pecans had become big business.

It grew bigger still, oddly enough, during the calamitous years of the Great Depression. This was especially true in San Antonio, where two forces converged in the mid-1920s that in time would change the industry and trigger a memorable protest against horrific working conditions and political paternalism.

The disruptive power of the Mexican Revolution sent thou-sands of people fleeing across the border in search of sanctuary, many of them destined for the Alamo City. What they found instead was a purgatory in the making. Settling on the city's west and south sides, finding shelter in any number of its "corrals" and shacks that had no running water or other utilities, they were mired in a pestilential environment, enduring the pressures of ris-ing population density and struggling to find work. Their very large numbers made matters worse. The overabundance of un-skilled, cheap labor depressed wages already sinking in response to the early stages of the depression.

This economic and social catastrophe had a curious impact on the pecan industry. Because wages were so low, shelling corporations in San Antonio (but nowhere else) set aside their mechanized shelling equipment and shifted to hand labor. Leading this regressive move was the city's Southern Pecan Shelling Company, which Joe Freeman and Louis Seligmann founded in 1926 with a $50,000 investment. The company rapidly dominated the market, Julia Blackwelder argues in *Women of the Depression* (1984), because its reliance on hand labor drastically cut its overhead and was thus "an inducement to expansion of the industry." Cheaper and more profitable still was its subsequent innovation, the contract system of shelling, in which the corporation supplied the pecans "to individuals or families, who were paid $0.06 to $0.08 a pound to shell the nuts at home." Even that skimpy scale did not hold up. By the late 1930s hand labor was getting a mere four cents a pound. The Southern, meanwhile, was raking in profits hand over fist. It generated $700,000 in sales in 1930, a figure that by 1936 had more than quadrupled. To justify this stunning discrepancy between plummeting wages and soaring profits, a San Antonio operator struck a paternalistic note. "If [shellers] have $5.00 they stay out and spend it," George Azar asserted. "You can't make a Mexican work a whole week if they have money enough to live on."

It must have come as something of a shock to him when a mass of these so-called idlers rose up in 1934 and 1935, and more forcefully in 1938, and tried to shut down the companies to which they apparently owed so much. These strikes, and the emergence of their electric leader, Emma Tenayuca, have been much and well told. Tenayuca's magnetism, the shellers' determination, the Southern's intransigence, the police department's belligerence— these gave birth to a tension in which the lines of political power and social prejudice in San Antonio were vividly manifest and, if only momentarily, disputed.

The moment passed all too quickly. By 1940, stricter enforcement of the Fair Labor Standards Act boosted wages, but the Southern and other companies simply reconverted to shelling machines and in a matter of months drastically cut the workforce from a peak of 10,000 to 800. Reduced, too, was the young woman who had done so much to publicize the pecan worker's plight: an avowed communist, Tenayuca was harassed and arrested, and later red-baited out of town.

Years later she would return to San Antonio and live in quiet retirement. Her death in the summer of 1999 marked an apotheosis of sorts. Her reputation thoroughly burnished, Tenayuca received a hero's funeral in San Fernando Cathedral. During the service, there was a procession of gifts to honor her contributions to the community. "A simple of basket of pecans," writer Jan Jarboe Russell reported, "stirred the most emotion." Its affective appeal was tied to its sacramental quality, the basket a communion offering. In making the profane sacred, this simple memento inverted the narration of oppression associated with the nut and the brutal industry it once sustained. Through Tenayuca, the pecan and a people had been liberated.

A GOOD EARTH

For the Birds

The timing could not have been more ironic or instructive: no sooner had the news hit the wires in late June 1995 that the House Appropriations Committee had voted out a bill sharply cutting the scientific research and environmental regulatory powers of the U.S. Department of the Interior than word came of an extremely unusual sighting of a juvenile aplomado falcon in the Rio Grande Valley. This species has been so endangered that decades earlier the authoritative birder Roger Tory Peterson noted it was "very rare" to catch even a glimpse of it in its South Texas habitat. None had been spotted since the 1950s, and the last known breeding pair in the United States had been seen in 1952 in New Mexico. But there one was, diving and returning to its perch atop a utility pole near the Port of Brownsville, in deep South Texas.

That the falcon had survived long enough to practice its survival skills was something of a minor miracle, a reflection of its provenance that was a complex weave of public and private activism, of money and science. Raised and released by Peregrine

Fund biologists, in a project jointly underwritten by federal conservation dollars emanating from the Interior Department and
private foundations, its young life was protected under the Endangered Species Act. Here, then, was a sanguine example of the
beneficence of committed human stewardship. That this kind of
outreach was to have been terminated at the hands of Republican
congressional cost-cutters spoke volumes. On the appropriate relationship between humanity and environment, the federal government was at odds with itself.

This internal conflict in itself was not odd. The clash between
conservationists and those who deride them—such as those
lawmakers and their constituents who assert that human needs
should be paramount and uncontested—finds its source in an
ancient text, that of Genesis. In its first chapter, stark differences
emerge between the status God assigns to the human population
and that he assigns to the animals. Humanity was created to have
dominion "over the fish of the sea, and over the fowl of the air, and
over the cattle, and over all the earth," including over "every
creeping thing," we learn in Genesis 1:26. Two verses later, the
language of dominance is tempered so that although humans are
to "subdue" the land, as divine creatures we are also commanded
to "replenish" the world we use. What Genesis offered was an
uneasy balance between dominion and conservation, control and
stewardship, a balance we have been struggling to maintain ever
since.

Since the late nineteenth century, when the principles of conservation—indeed the word itself—became part of our political
lexicon, Americans have battled over the importance of an idea

that demanded they rein in their avarice, slow down their consumption of natural resources, and work to restore a cut-over terrain. When conservationists such as George Bird Grinnell, founding editor of *Field and Stream*, President Theodore Roosevelt, and famed naturalist John Muir proposed and enacted legislation that established a series of national forests and national parks, wildlife refuges, and bird sanctuaries, they did so in hopes of setting aside a portion of the American landscape from the rapacious energy that the Industrial Revolution had unleashed.

While many of their contemporaries shared this Edenic vision and its faith in the human capacity to regenerate a wounded land, others furiously opposed its application, believing that nothing should restrain the economic impulse that underlay the capitalist enterprise. If the pursuit of wealth meant that mining would take place in the Grand Canyon, or that the geothermal geysers of Yellowstone would be tapped and drained, or that ancient stands of California redwoods would fall to the ax, so be it. Such actions, after all, were consistent with the biblical injunction to subjugate the earth.

In the mid-1990s, subjugation was uppermost in the minds of legislators in the Republican-dominated nation's capitol. As House Speaker Newt Gingrich and his Republican peers moved to eradicate such watchdog agencies as the U.S. Bureau of Mines, slash the appropriations for other federal environmental organizations, gut the Endangered Species Act, and thereby deny ecologists the opportunity to analyze the complexities of and plan for habitat restoration, they aborted their party's allegiance to the conservationist principles for which Teddy Roosevelt stood. For these latter-day Republicans, nothing could be gained from the creation of an American Eden.

The near decimation of the aplomado falcon suggested otherwise. Almost wiped out by the indiscriminate use of pesticides and the wanton destruction of its indigenous habitat, it was being revived by human action. This multifaceted endeavor cut across the traditional divide between environmentalists, ranchers, and developers and created a meeting of the minds that Interior Secretary Bruce Babbitt had praised during his March 1998 visit to Laguna Atascosa National Wildlife Refuge in Cameron County, Texas, site of the falcon restoration work. Peering through a telescope and catching a glimpse of a lone falcon, he saluted the cooperative efforts of groups often thought to be in opposition to one another. "That bird," he told reporters, is a "powerful oneliner. In South Texas, real westerners say, 'bring me your endangered species.'"

That Babbitt gazed on but one aplomado falcon indicated just how insecure its status was in 1995. Since then, however, it has staged a remarkable comeback. The key to this has been the development of the Safe Harbor Program, in which the federal government grants private landowners incentives to manage their property in ways that benefit endangered flora and fauna. Under this plan, the Peregrine Fund began to reintroduce falcons on some of the more than 1.6 million acres that South Texas ranchers had dedicated to the conservation of the aplomado falcon, with spectacular results. By the spring of 2002, more than 800 captive-bred falcons had been released in the wild, and upward of thirty-seven breeding pairs had survived to fledge more than ninety-two young. This data was so encouraging that the U.S. Fish and Wildlife Service and the Peregrine Fund expanded the restoration project to West Texas and planned to return the aplomado to its historic range in southern New Mexico.

These efforts have been worth every penny because they remind us of the divine wisdom of humanity's earthly stewardship. It has only been through such a concerted, conservationist impulse that we are able to witness what was once a common sight in South Texas: hosts of adult falcons teaching their fledglings to fly and hunt. With their signature cinnamon breast flashing overhead, they wheel, dip, and dive through the humid, shimmering air of the Rio Grande Valley, a command performance.

Rio Grande Blues

Late every summer, South Texans begin to yearn for a hurricane. This is an understandable (if dangerous) impulse, sparked by a brush country sizzling in the hot sun, rapidly shrinking water levels in regional reservoirs, and fissures cracking open the hard-baked terrain. Emblematic of these signals of environmental distress is the imperiled state of the once mighty Rio Grande, which runs more than 1,200 miles from its headwaters in the Rocky Mountains to the Gulf of Mexico. It has seen better days. Much better.

In some segments, its flow has become so pitiful that the river has been reduced to a series of puddles. In other stretches, tributaries give it a bit of a push. But that natural increase in speed and volume is sullied by the artificial boost it receives from urban water-treatment plant discharge and factory effluent. Symptomatic of its sorry state, the Rio Grande no longer reaches the Gulf, unable even to surmount Boca Chica, a low sandbar at its mouth.

More degrading still are the politics that have wrapped around the river and helped suffocate its life. Granted, they have always been complicated, as befits a river that serves as an international boundary. But the political complications escalated in the first years of the twenty-first century. In the spring of 2002, for example, American irrigators, a heavily subsidized class of water users in good part responsible for the river's diminished flow, demanded that the Bush administration force Mexico to release 1.5 million acre-feet of water stored in international reservoirs. This vast amount was owed to U.S. consumers under terms of the 1944 U.S.-Mexico Water Treaty. That summer's negotiations proved difficult, however, and when a resolution was announced in late June 2002—Mexico agreed to release 91,000 acre-feet—all hell broke loose. At least it did on the American side of the border. Denouncing the agreement as nothing but an insulting token, irrigators linked up with state and congressional politicians to clamor for a better deal.

The ruckus worked in this respect. Rep. Henry Bonilla (R-San Antonio) and Sen. Kay Bailey Hutchison (R-Texas), while sitting on a joint House–Senate conference committee haggling over a supplemental spending bill, pulled off a bit of legislative legerdemain; they snagged an extra $10 million for South Texas irrigators to offset some of the losses they faced due to drought.

That was not the end of the maneuvering. Hoping to jack up the debate over the Rio Grande's paltry flow, four Rio Grande Valley congressmen let loose a provocative press release in mid-July designed to roil the waters. Alleging that the Bush administration had "sold South Texas down the river," Reuben Hinojosa (D-Mission), Solomon Ortiz (D-Corpus Christi), Sylvester Reyes (D-El Paso), and Ciro Rodriguez (D-San Antonio), whose district

snakes down to the Rio Grande Valley, declared that an aggressive
Congress had to force Mexico back to the bargaining table. "If the
President is not going to exercise leadership," Reyes warned the
Associated Press, "we will."

The tactic was a simple piece of high-stakes diplomacy. If
Mexico failed to release the acre-feet of water it owed Texas farmers and ranchers, the four congressional representatives vowed to
submit legislation to bottle up Mexico-bound water from the
Colorado River (which is also governed under the 1944 Water
Treaty). There was also talk of rerouting the impounded waters
into the Rio Grande Basin.

This piece of election-year grandstanding had little chance of
success. The Republicans, who controlled the U.S. House of Representatives, were well aware just how slim the four representatives' hold over that body was, and they had no interest in allowing such a volatile measure to secure a public hearing. They
recognized that the potential blow-back might engulf the president and his party in the run-up to the 2002 midterm elections.
Equally chimerical that summer was the notion that Valley agricultural interests would be able to capture the acre-feet potentially
held hostage in Colorado River reservoirs. The cost to build
diversionary channels or pipelines would break the bank and
require years to construct, offering not even a trickle of aid to
those thirsty for a more robust streamflow.

Yet the water fight had its point. Equitable access to the river
is essential to maintaining the Rio Grande's binational economies. But the river's waters will be ever more difficult to secure
and distribute as a result of the Valley's sustained population
boom. As of the summer of 2002 it was home to a crowded 2.4

million people, with no end in sight. If not addressed, this demo-graphic situation on both sides of the border spells disaster for the region and the river. A high quality of human life and riparian health will require careful analysis, realistic reforms, and intense investment in the built and natural landscapes. To rehabilitate the Rio Grande will require the kind of long-term commitment that politicians, hooked on the quick fix, have been loath to pursue.

Although unlikely, they must adopt a new strategy, the first step of which would be to rewrite the 1944 Water Treaty. It was negotiated and signed at a very different point in the history of its two signatories. Mexico had hoped the treaty would shore up its political independence, reduce reliance on U.S.-based water pur-veyors, and encourage economic growth along its northern border. The United States sought to promote southwestern development and enhance relations with an important hemispheric ally during World War Two. In the short term, both nations got what they wanted because there was enough water to go around.

That is no longer the case, as demand far exceeds supply. The only way to alter this is by revising how Americans and Mexicans think about the river as a river. Legal scholar Raúl Sánchez has argued that the 1944 treaty often conceives of water as a "national" product. For instance, the San Juan River, the Rio Grande's sec-ond largest southern tributary, is a "Mexican" river, and therefore its waters may be fully captured in Mexico. Such designations are "contrary to the modern trend in international river law toward a basinwide approach to international watercourse issues," Sánchez notes. Such an approach would require a new water treaty that would allow for a more sophisticated, environmentally sensitive approach to watershed management.

Yet to be successful, any new treaty must also tackle the real costs of agricultural subsidies. Like their peers throughout the American West, Valley farmers of sugarcane and citrus are subsidized by the federal government in their disproportionate use of the river's streamflow; their consumption of 75 percent of water supplies produces a meager $500 million in value. By contrast, the Valley's urban-industrial economy's 25 percent share manufactures a robust $10 billion. This unbalanced and unjustifiable policy "makes no sense," Rice University political scientist Dagobert Brito commented in the *Houston Chronicle*. "Water would not be scarce . . . if it were allocated in an economically rational manner."

It would be more plentiful, too, if a new treaty required rigorous conservation by urban and rural consumers. Those who live in Brownsville, for example, use 229 gallons of water a day; in Laredo the per capita figure is 200, in McAllen 205, in El Paso 188, and in Del Rio an astounding 316. By contrast, San Antonians in 2002 used a meager 126 gallons. How were they able to conserve so much? By plugging household and urban pipelines, sealing agricultural canals, installing low-flow toilets and showers, and spraying recycled water on landscapes, as well as by raising water prices. A similar strategy would produce similar results for the profligate Rio Grande Valley.

If new conservation regulations were embedded in a fully revamped water treaty between Mexico and the United States, the document would usher in a more sustainable future for the borderlands and make it less likely that Texans in the Valley would have to look to Mother Nature to bail them out.

Going Coastal

The annual hurricane season, from June to November, reminds residents of the Texas Gulf Coast just how precarious their toehold is on this low-lying landscape. Most frightening are the storm surges, the greatest of which leveled Galveston in 1900, killing more than 6,000 people. Yet even smaller storms can spin off killer tornadoes and damaging downbursts of hail, leading to wrack and ruin.

No wonder the residents of Corpus Christi keep a weather eye in two directions—south, to watch for the swirling buildup of ominous cloud formations over the bathtub-warm waters of the Bay of Campeche; and north, in case a tropical depression should whip toward this sea-level city of 250,000. Its citizens have to be able to gauge when to squeeze into the thick stream of cars inching up Interstate 37 to San Antonio, 125 miles away.

Although Corpus has only had to evacuate once since Hurricane Celia smashed into it in August 1970, splintering its infrastructure and flooding its central core, memories of that massive storm and the destruction left in its wake still haunt the town. So in late August 1999, when the National Weather Service predicted that Bret, a quick-moving, category four hurricane, would make landfall in and around the coastal bend, the prediction triggered a rush to flee. "We went through Celia," one harried resident muttered while hammering plywood over her home's windows, "and that is why we are leaving."

She was not alone. More than 30,000 automobiles clogged the two northbound lanes of the interstate linking Corpus Christi and San Antonio, turning it into a parking lot. Television-station helicopters beamed back rain-streaked images of what appeared to be a 100-mile-long white ribbon of headlights. Under normal conditions, the trip takes less than three hours, but on that Saturday evening it took more than eight. In the end, the evacuation was unnecessary: Bret veered west, going ashore some sixty miles south of Corpus and pounding the least densely populated portion of the South Texas coastline.

All had not been for naught. The car-choked exodus prompted state and local politicians and transportation officials to devise new evacuation plans, which include reversing IH-37's southbound lanes to convert the freeway into an extended four-lane escape route. Should another hurricane sweep across the Gulf to threaten Corpus, its inhabitants will reach San Antonio, their inland safe harbor, more quickly.

The growing awareness that Corpus Christi might serve as San Antonio's deepwater port initially forged the two cities' tight relations—an environmental and human connection established by the railroad in the late nineteenth century. Like their peers throughout the United States, South Texas urban boosters were convinced that in a railroad's wake new towns would spring up, communities would be transformed, and new work and wealth would galvanize economies large and small. Because of the resources its construction consumed, and the impact it would have on natural and built landscapes, the railroad was the preeminent symbol of the progress the Industrial Revolution could be expected to produce.

These glittering possibilities sparked a series of unsuccessful mid-nineteenth-century plans to lay down tracks between the two ambitious communities. The motivation of those planning these lines was understandable. Since the late 1840s, mule-drawn wagons and carts had plodded north and south in a rough, slow transit that limited the extent and significance of the two towns' commercial interaction. Although a rail connection would offer more rapid, consistent, and valuable trade, locating the financing to underwrite the project was difficult. So difficult, in fact, that Uriah Lott, the tireless promoter of what became the San Antonio and Aransas Pass Railroad (SAP), resorted to some creative financing to build the rail line. He cobbled together a bit of capital, begged for supplies, and relied on a lot of credit, a tenuous scheme that somehow succeeded. No wonder citizens in both towns were so enthusiastic (and relieved) when the final spikes were hammered into place in late October 1886. To mark "the advent of the iron horse," Corpus Christi threw a "grand barbecue" and invited all South Texans to attend, the *Austin Statesman* reported. San Antonians were particularly encouraged to come so that they could "fraternize" with their new neighbors. Taking advantage of the five-dollar, three-day pass, many in the Alamo City rode the rails to the seaport, initiating a new era in the two cities' relationship.

Among these were boosters eager to corral what they claimed was their city's "Tributary Territory." Its 1888 boundaries, according to the *San Antonio Express*, were set within a "triangle south of San Antonio to the Mexican border, formed by the Southern Pacific to Eagle Pass and the San Antonio and Aransas Pass railways to Corpus Christi, and pierced almost through its centre by the International and Great Northern Railway to Laredo." Framed in this cross-hatching of tracks was a vast terrain comprising more than 36,000 square miles of rich and fertile land.

Everywhere within that broad swath, life and labor were being reorganized. SAP investors had gambled that, as the line worked south from San Antonio to Floresville, then Beeville, and finally Corpus Christi, it would open up this verdant "stock country." Its horses, cattle, sheep, goats, and horses would be herded onto cars for shipment to San Antonio markets or those in more distant midwestern and northeastern urban centers. The owners hoped as well to tap what one report called "the incipient cotton culture springing up east of the Nueces [River], and the vegetable growing in Nueces County." More desirable still was the access the railroad offered to the shipping lines that plied between Corpus Christi and national and international ports. From this one railroad there was considerable money to be made.

But when the final pile was driven into the Corpus Christi reefs, and passenger and freight traffic commenced operations, a serious environmental complication nearly scuttled the region's giddy economic prospects. Aransas Pass, through which the famed Morgan Lines of New York and other freighters entered Corpus Christi Bay, periodically shoaled over, leading shippers to cut back their service to the port. Stabilizing "a deep water entrance at Aransas Pass is certainly a most pressing [question] for Southwest Texas," the *San Antonio Express* warned in 1888, signaling that the once landlocked city now understood how important the coastal city had become to its aspirations. South Texas congressional representatives and local politicians argued successfully for federal funds to dredge and shore up the silted-over channel. Beginning in 1879 and accelerating after the SAP was built, nearly $550,000 was appropriated for this maintenance program through Congress's annual Harbor and Bridges Acts.

This was good money well spent, all agreed. Especially convinced were those San Antonians who had been lucky enough to travel to Corpus. There they quickly acclimated to their role as Gulf Coast tourists. They romped in tepid bay waters, strolled along the white strand, and gorged on fresh-caught seafood and shellfish. Suntanned and sated, they headed home, perhaps carrying gastronomic delights iced down in the baggage cars. Soon San Antonio's restaurants faced skyrocketing demand for gulf oysters, a unexpected result of the landlocked city's newly acquired opening to the sea.

Grazing Rules

It was through the eyes of an Italian journalist that I saw anew the stark beauty and rich agricultural legacy of Bandera County. In early July 2001, Eduardo Vigna, a leading columnist for Milan's *Corriere della Sere*, came to South Texas on a U.S. State Department–sponsored visit. He was interested in how agricultural regions like the Hill Country were being affected by globalization, and how they had responded to the often dramatic transformations that accompanied the migration of work to Third World countries. I'm not sure why I was fortunate enough to be asked on the daylong jaunt, or why Vigna did all the driving, but I was delighted to join State Department host Andrea Terrell as Vigna took us back into a very complicated past.

Some of the historic complexities became clear as we headed up u.s. 281, swung west on Loop 1604, and turned north and west on State Highway 16, aptly named Bandera Road. Everywhere we saw markers of San Antonio's rapid post–World War Two population surge—sprawling housing divisions, auto dealerships, and retail centers built up along the major arteries heading out of town. Given Vigna's interest in the impact of new economies on old landscapes, he was understandably intrigued by remnants of ranching at the margins of this burgeoning city. Here and there we saw a horse grazing outside a six-foot wooden privacy fence, now the standard demarcation of suburban space.

Just how far those fences stretched was surprising. It was not until we passed Helotes, roughly twenty miles out of town, and began to climb to higher elevations, that they slipped from our vision. Then we began to chat about the historic relationship between the Edwards Plateau and those who lived in what would become San Antonio.

Native American peoples had long made good use of the plateau's river valleys and creekbeds. Archeological evidence dug up in and around the headwaters of Olmos, Salado, Panther Springs, and Leon Creeks, tributaries of the San Antonio River, reveals "semi-permanent settlements" dating back to at least 9200 B.C.E. Those who inhabited these sites in the years before the Spanish arrived conducted seasonal hunting expeditions up into the plateau, where bison and deer were plentiful. They lived within and moved between the watersheds of the region's major rivers and participated in trade networks that extended from present-day New Mexico to the Gulf Coast and eastern Texas.

Their folkways and economies began to disappear with the late-seventeenth-century arrival of the Lipan Apache and the Spanish, and they were fully cleared away with the mid-nineteenth-century Anglo and German introduction of cattle, goat, and sheep along plateau rivers such as the Medina and the Guadalupe. The development of a set of urban market forces reinforced these alterations.

Frederick Law Olmsted sensed these transforming economic trends as he traversed the hilly terrain in the early 1850s. Beguiled by the low "montaines" that rolled north from San Antonio, Olmsted believed this rough landscape was perfect pasture. "The natural use of the country was, palpably, for grazing, and that, sheep grazing. We could hardly refrain from expecting, on each bleak hill, to startle a black-faced flock, and see a plaided, silent, long-legged shepherd appear on the scene." To realize this romantic vision would require an enormous effort on the part of migrants who, like the German settlers Olmsted so admired, entered the Hill Country in the 1840s, and who destroyed competing wildlife and helped other human claimants to its riches. Bears, panthers, and Indians had to go.

Their eradication was not complete until after the American Civil War, and Bandera County's early history reflected this slow evolution. Founded in the early 1850s, the sparsely settled county grew slowly around the milling of indigenous cypress stands rooted deep in the Medina River valley; it was not until the 1870s that its economy matured and its population expanded. Ranchers began to raise herds of cattle, then sheep and goats in even larger numbers, and by the 1880s wool was the county's single most important product. The human population, though always smaller than the animals it tended, grew as well, from 649 in 1870 to 2,158 in 1880; by the next decade it had reached 3,795.

This steady growth was tied to economic and environmental changes that reinforced San Antonio's late-nineteenth-century designation as the most important regional marketplace. Before the Civil War, for instance, many ranchers had hauled the annual wool shear on wagons to the coastal ports of Indianola or Port Lavaca, from which it was shipped to textile mills in New England. Poor transportation and the extended distance from market put Texas ranchers at a distinct disadvantage when it came time to sell their clip. Some of those disadvantages disappeared in the late 1860s when Thomas Clayton Frost developed freight service between San Antonio and the Gulf ports, and contracted with other teamsters to haul in wool and other products from Bandera and surrounding counties. Soon thereafter, Frost opened the well-stocked T.C. Frost Company on the city's Main Plaza, by whose provisions he hoped to corral much of the hinterland's wool production. By offering wool producers credit in his store in exchange for the right to market their shear, and by opening a storage facility to keep the wool until market prices rose, Frost stabilized his customers' cash flow and boosted his profit margins. His business acumen had much to do with making wool a staple in the postwar economy of San Antonio, Bandera, and the surrounding Hill Country.

Restructuring rural trade routes and economic energies were not Frost's only accomplishments. He and others like him also had to respond to an environmentally driven shift in the siting of the South Texas livestock business. There had been warnings in the late 1860s about the impact of intensive grazing on the region's grasslands, specifically on the Rio Grande Plain; of the 100,000 sheep in Texas denoted in the 1850 U.S. Census, half were located south and west of San Antonio. By the early 1880s, the Rio

Grande Plain contained nearly 2.5 million sheep and goats (triple the number of cattle), and within four years the number bulged to nearly 4 million. The land could not sustain such spectacular numbers of herbivores, and many sheep owners, seeking greener terrain, trailed their animals north into the Edwards Plateau or farther west into the Trans-Pecos region. By 1900, the transition was complete, with more than 1.5 million sheep grazing the Edwards.

Bandera kept pace with these changes, much as it did when plateau ranchers turned Angora goats out to pasture on the thin limestone soils. In 1910 there were more than 73,000 goats in the county, and by 1930 the figure had swelled to nearly 129,000. But these impressive numbers mask an important decline: the human population in Bandera, as elsewhere, had begun to drop. Because ranching now consumed greater amounts of land and other resources, farmers had difficulty sustaining themselves, and some moved farther west or to Austin, New Braunfels, San Antonio, and other nearby cities. Peaking at 5,332 people in 1900, Bandera's population fell to 4,001 in 1920, and then to 3,784 a decade later. The rural boom was over, followed by a downward spiral that intensified with the Great Depression and continued through the immediate post–World War Two era.

It was not through this landscape of decline that Eduardo Vigna drove in 2001, for something striking has occurred in Bandera since the 1970s. The population has eclipsed prewar levels: in 2001, more than 18,500 called the county home, representing a robust 67 percent increase since 1990. The number of housing starts has risen dramatically, new schools have been built, and the county's expanding tax base has generated funding for much-needed upgrades in the countywide infrastructure.

The source of these energetic developments is also new—a hint of which is contained in the fact that Bandera County is now part of the San Antonio Metropolitan Area. This designation, the U.S. Census Bureau's shorthand for urban sprawl, is keyed to two factors. A county will only be included in a metropolitan area if 75 percent of its workforce is nonagricultural and if 15 percent or more of its residents travel daily to the central city for their employment. Beginning in the 1970s, Bandera absorbed an influx of automobile-dependent residents who each day navigated a 100-mile round-trip commute to San Antonio. How ironic that the economic and social changes their presence has brought to the county effaced the very rural landscape these urbanites apparently hungered to live in.

That was what Vigna noticed most of all—the power of a regional urban system to transform built and natural landscapes. When we arrived that bright, clear morning in Bandera, for example, we met up with Mark Tobin, who guided us through his family's ranch and introduced us to other longtime ranching families. Although Vigna's conversations with them touched on the grazing industry's demise in the face of changes in global agricultural economics, his interviewees also spoke movingly of a devil's bargain they had made. To underwrite what was left of their operations so that their children might inherit something of the family's heritage, many had sold off tracts to homebuilders or individual families, creating a patchwork of new land uses that are crowding out older ones.

Judging by the sluggish flow of twilight traffic we rolled past as we headed back to San Antonio, this churning of real estate will surely intensify. None of us missed the significance of the road's most ubiquitous, outbound vehicle: the Chevy Suburban.

WATERMARKS

Flood of Memories

At dawn, rescuers found an adolescent clinging to a tree on South Flores Street, holding a five-year-old child high on his shoulders above the still dangerous and murky floodwaters. The pair had apparently clambered into this rough sanctuary sometime after midnight on September 10, 1921, when a thunderous surge swept through San Antonio's west side. For more than five hours, the older youth, whom the press later identified simply as a "12 year old Mexican boy," had been "battered black and blue by floating wreckage." Surviving this bruising ordeal, local newspapers cheered, was a mark of his "outstanding heroism."

A day earlier, no one would have imagined the need for such heroics. The summer had been typical for south-central Texas, each day as dry and as hot as the next. So on September 9, when light rains swept across the region, reviving pastures, lawns, and gardens and dropping temperatures into the high eighties, there was a sigh of relief: not only had these "most timely showers" put an end to a "prolonged drouth," the *San Antonio Express* reported, but they had done so without damaging crops or flooding low-lying neighborhoods.

Over the next twenty-four hours, however, violent thunderstorms pounded the region, dropping more than twenty inches of rain in some areas and triggering flash floods of immense power and destructive force. San Antonio was particularly hard hit: its rainfall measured but seven and a half inches, yet most fell within a few hours when a storm cell stalled just north of the city, concentrating a downburst over the watershed of the San Antonio River. Later that evening, its major tributaries, the San Pedro, Alazán, and Martínez Creeks, burst over their banks, becoming "swift torrents" of destruction. They ripped through the crowded barrios of the west and south sides of the city, sweeping so many houses away that no official tally was kept. Left behind were fifty-foot piles of debris. The floodwaters also killed more than fifty people, most of whom were sucked into the raging creeks during the early hours of the morning. Finding their bodies was no easy task. For the rest of the week, able-bodied civilians and soldiers were stationed on downstream bridges to spot, and then attempt to retrieve, corpses entangled in the sodden detritus.

A somewhat less ghastly job awaited those who would clean up from the flooding associated with Olmos Creek, which cut through the city's north and east sides. It had powered over its banks around midnight, rushing into adjacent neighborhoods and urban parks and flushing out residents and campers. When its crest smashed into the San Antonio River, it forced a five- to ten-foot wall of water through the central business district, inundating the bottom floors of most office buildings, damaging a considerable portion of the commercial inventory, tearing up miles of street pavement, and weakening or washing away the structural integrity of the city's many bridges. Located downtown, too, were the sources of San Antonio's basic utilities—water, electricity, and telephone—which were consequently shut down for several days. Ruptured fuel storage tanks added to the mess, spreading an oil slick several miles long and equally wide. Although early estimates of the overall damage were set at $3 million, by the time the cleanup was completed several months later, the costs had escalated to more than $4 million. Certainly San Antonians knew that by any form of measurement—by the height of the floodwaters, the number of deaths and injuries, or the financial costs—the 1921 flood was the greatest disaster in the city's history.

Yet the flood's impact went well beyond any specific tally of human loss or physical destruction. Indeed, of greater consequence was the community's response to the critical question of how to control future floods. The initial response was swift and telling. The press rooms of the rival *San Antonio Express* and *San Antonio Light* had not been pumped dry when each newspaper editorialized fervently in support of a citywide network of canals and the erection of a detention dam spanning the Olmos Valley to prevent damaging floods. That was the least the citizenry could do, for the "mass of wreckage" left in the flood's wake was mute testimony that "the elements, when loosed from the gates of hell, are no respecters of persons, class or creed." It was high time for San Antonians to recognize this fact of nature, the *Express* trumpeted. "The storm waters must be controlled," for only then could the city be rehabilitated.

But exactly which storm waters most needed to be controlled, and thus which portions of the community would undergo rehabilitation, would be decided in the political arena. Flood-control politics proved integral to the city's development through the first half of the twentieth century. When completed in 1927, for example, the 1,900-foot Olmos Dam helped articulate the city's land-use patterns and redefined its spatial design. The dam's mere presence intensified the central core's already established economic functions by encouraging once-wary financiers to invest heavily in the city's postflood downtown skyline. The 1920s construction boom produced some of the city's finest and largest buildings, from the Smith-Young Tower to the Scottish Rite Temple and the Medical Arts Building. The dam also made it possible to conceive, and then develop, the much-ballyhooed Riverwalk. Without it there would be few tourists strolling along its (now) placid waters, tourists who have become one of the mainstays of San Antonio's modern economy. Because of these ramifications, the Olmos Dam is arguably the single most important public works project in the city's history.

But the dam was also a failure, in the sense that the decision to build it depended upon a disturbing and remarkably skewed distribution of public benefits in one of America's poorest big cities. That is not what San Antonio's Anglo leadership announced, of course, when it floated a $3 million bond issue to underwrite the dam, ensuring the central business district's bright future. It simultaneously voiced a commitment to establish a flood-control plan for the waterlogged barrios. This action, civic leaders proclaimed, was only just, for the vast majority of those who had died in the 1921 flood had been Hispanics who lived along dangerous creeks well outside the proposed dam's protective zone. As the national publication *The Survey*, a Progressive Era reform organ, noted, the stage was set for the city to do more than build prosaic storm sewers. By sweeping away the dense tracts of "rude shacks, built in a hit or miss manner," the 1921 flood gave San Antonio a perfect "opportunity for bettering the lives and sanitary conditions of the Mexican population." Out of an immense tragedy could come some social good.

No such luck. Concerned ultimately (and only) with the reconstruction of the commercial core, the urban elite ignored the legendary drainage, housing, and sanitation problems confronting those who lived on the city's west and south sides; their plight was theirs alone. Nothing captures these disparities more perfectly than the paired announcements coming from city council in August 1924: at the same time it released millions of dollars to fund the Olmos Dam, the council voted to spend a meager $6,000 to cut brush along the San Pedro and Alazán Creeks. This remarkable discrepancy in financial investment and flood prevention technology would continue for the next fifty years. The management of San Antonio's floodwaters, as with so much else, was channeled along sharply etched ethnic divisions and class lines.

The dire consequences of this discriminatory policy resurfaced continuously. In the 1930s, a series of murderous floods cascaded through the barrios while downtown remained high and dry. When a massive storm stalled over San Antonio in June 1946, the Olmos Dam did what it was built to do, but on the west side ten people lost their lives and thousands more were left homeless in the wake of rampaging floodwaters. The same results occurred when a punishing storm in June 1951 churned up the Alazán and Martínez Creeks—called "those old trouble spots" in one newspaper account—killing three residents.

This pattern would repeat itself until the early 1970s, when dramatic changes occurred in the city's political hierarchy. These were triggered when Justice Department–ordered electoral reforms compelled west side representation on the city council, breaking its control by the white-dominated Good Government League. This encouraged the rise of Communities Organized for Public Services (COPS) and other successful grassroots political coalitions whose first goal was to stop the deadly floods. Only when pushed by the formerly disenfranchised did San Antonio finally muster the political will to tap into federal dollars, through Model Cities funding, and begin to build a network of broad concrete channels to defuse the long-standing threat the west side creeks had posed to the city's poorest citizens and neighborhoods. Participatory democracy had triumphed.

Its triumph, however, is mitigated by this damning reflection: it took the River City more than half a century to build the requisite infrastructure to make certain west side kids wouldn't have to scramble up a tree to escape becoming yet another flood fatality.

Wash Out

The man stood on the roof of his white pickup truck. Roiling over the truckbed was a swirl of water he had tried to drive through. But his engine had stalled halfway across the low-water crossing, and Salado Creek was rising fast. Frustrated and fearful, he shook his fist at television cameras hastily erected to capture yet another harrowing incident on that dark, wet day in October 1998. As if to underscore the obvious, he shouted above the river's roar, "San Antonio, you've got a flood problem!"

Amid a torrential downburst that spawned substantial flooding in early July 2002, the ubiquitous cameras caught yet another pickup. This time the truck was high and dry, but stranded nonetheless on the far side of a local stream whose force had ripped away a bridge. Its destruction left a neighborhood isolated, and in a plea for help one resident had taped a sign to his windshield: "Send Bridge."

These snapshots of the Great Floods of 1998 and 2002 attest to our enduring desire for unfettered mobility, our overweening ambition to transcend nature, and our unabashed faith in our technological prowess. And with every storm, nature undercuts our hubris, flattens our ambitions, and sweeps aside the human hold on South Texas.

We should have learned that lesson by now, but our flood management strategies reveal our unshakable desire for mastery of the elements, as does our haste to rebuild every damaged bridge, repave each pockmarked highway, and construct more flood-control channels and dams. But no matter how many millions of dollars we invest in the creation of what we hope will prove a more durable flood-prevention infrastructure—currently there is an estimated $1 billion worth of proposed projects—we still will not elevate ourselves much above the cab of a flooding pickup.

So the good folks living in the Woodlawn Lake District of San Antonio will attest. The lake around which their neighborhood was built was originally constructed as a flood-retention pond for Alazán Creek. In recent years, the lake has been dredged, and the tributaries' banks were deepened and widened to carry greater volume. All that effort went for naught on July 1, 2002. That night, as many area residents sat down to dinner, the skies opened up and upward of nine inches of rain fell in less than two hours. A feeder into the creek overran its banks and streamed onto Kampmann Avenue, which collected the swift-moving water and carried it south. Its force began to move parked cars down the winding street, and as the wet wall rose and spilled into yards, it increased in height and energy. By 7 P.M. residents were reporting that water had seeped into their homes, and at their peak floodwaters were waist-deep, damaging hundreds of abodes in the middle-class neighborhood. As a discouraged Paolo Christadoro told a reporter, "I grew up in this neighborhood and thought we couldn't flood because we're on high ground."

Yet there is precious little upland in a flood basin, and that's what San Antonio is. Our geography, geology, and climate create a unique landscape defined by the overlapping boundaries of several environmental and physical zones. Tucked under the Hill Country, whose southern, downward edge is known as the Balcones Escarpment, San Antonio sprawls across the transition between the Great Plains and the Gulf Coastal Plain. It is positioned as well within an important climatic variable, the shift from the humid east and the arid west. That gives us front-row seats from which to watch as cold-weather fronts collide with warm, subtropical Gulf air masses, producing astonishingly violent storms. When the rains slant down and strike the rock-hard hills, the runoff races through cuts in the limestone escarpment and sweeps into San Antonio (and New Braunfels, San Marcos, and Austin). South-central Texas is not called Flash-Flood Alley for nothing.

Despite this profound evidence of nature's power, the city and county have been fixated on a set of last-ditch initiatives to gain the upper hand through highly touted, regional flood-management plans. The most recent, released during the summer of 2002, assumed that an even more heavily engineered watershed would somehow conform to human expectations and needs. Illusory, too, was the attempt to define our region along artificial political boundaries. No river system respects county lines or city limits. John

Wesley Powell, legendary head of the U.S. Geological Survey, recognized this geographical reality in his *Report on the Lands of the
Arid Region of the United States* (1878). The central problem of the
Trans-Mississippi West, the one-armed, former Union major asserted after years of exploring the West's vast and rugged landscape, was water. To maintain life beyond the 98th meridian, he
urged that the "entire arid region be organized into natural hydro-
graphic districts," not around states, counties, or other political
designations. Although Powell hoped this spatial organization
would enable sustainable agriculture and community development, his notion of what he later called drainage districts—that
is, watersheds—remains strikingly relevant in a modern urban
flood plain. Put simply, he proposed that water should determine
the contours of the West's human ecology.

To think otherwise is dangerous, as San Antonio's water history has revealed. Until we learn to live with the environmental
realities peculiar to South Texas, we will be left like that driver
stranded atop his submerged pickup, shaking our fists at our fate.

Water Torture

Call them the jumping frogs of Bexar County. At the climax of a late June 1997 storm, dozens of the amphibians hip-hopped across our lake of a lawn, a riotous, vibrant, if ephemeral, celebration of the rejuvenation those ample rains brought to this once drought-stricken land. More durable evidence abounded: the reservoirs were overflowing, regional rivers such as the Colorado and the Comal and Guadalupe were running high and fast, and, as for the water levels in the Edwards Aquifer, it had been a long time since that vast underground cistern had been so full.

This richness of wet came at a cost. Accompanying the deluge were floods that swept away human life, ripped through housing, and tore up roads and bridges. In Bandera County alone, more than $9 million in infrastructure was damaged. Some of this devastation could not be repaired (how do you bring back those whose lives were lost?), but the material losses resulting from the floodwaters' turbulent power were restored or replaced, thanks to the surge of federal dollars that poured into south-central Texas.

The more than 200 residents in Bexar County who lost their homes, for example, became eligible for a series of grants and loans to help them rebuild. The region, in many ways, was flush.

That momentary plenty almost made me long for the catastrophic dry spell of 1995–96. Not that I had a hankering to wilt under a 100-degree sun for days on end or yearned to gaze once more on the charms of a scorched yard (though there was this distinct advantage: I never had to mow). But I missed the small social dramas and larger political battles the lengthy drought had engendered; they had entertained even as they illuminated our penchant for avoiding tough decisions about how to live in this semiarid landscape.

During those years we learned this truth: desperate times call for disparate measures, most of them comic. Divining rods made a comeback, and there were the usual earnest pleas for cloud-seeding experiments to lift the San Antonio region out of its meteorological black hole. In July 1996, a flock of local Baptists streamed outdoors for a prayer session exhorting the Almighty to spread his wet grace on this hard land. Others, afflicted by a bad case of precipitation envy, wanted to take matters into their own hands: tight water restrictions notwithstanding, they urged their neighbors to flood their yards to enhance local air quality. As one correspondent wrote in the *San Antonio Express-News*, "Green lawns take carbon dioxide and other pollutants out of the air and put oxygen into the air. Dead lawns don't." Clever schemes all, they reflected our deep need for help.

And help was on the way, local columnist Rick Casey had predicted that summer at the depth of our despair. It was a prediction based on a cosmic correlation between the degree of citizen agitation over water and the proximity of thunderheads. Each year, Casey wrote, the River City dries up by late August, sparking fights between thirsty consumers over a dwindling share of white gold, at which point the skies open up. It was a divine joke.

God must have been really laughing during the dog days of August 1997. While San Antonio Mayor Bill Thornton was in New Orleans slurping cafe au lait, snarfing a couple of beignets, and not incidentally filing a brief with the U.S. Court of Appeals for the Fifth Circuit to overturn federal judge Lucius Bunton's latest order for tighter regulations on pumping from the Edwards Aquifer, light showers swept the region. Temperatures cooled.

But not the political temper. Thornton continued to fume over Judge Bunton's order. While confident that the conservative New Orleans appeals court would overturn Bunton's ruling—a confidence the court upheld when the following May, on a split vote, it struck it down—Thornton lambasted the very idea of a "regulator in robes" forcing aquifer users to turn off the spigot. Even as the mayor acknowledged the wealth of data that led Bunton to declare a water emergency—total discharge from the aquifer had exceeded total recharge over the past three years, suggesting that a "bad water line" might contaminate the underground reservoir—he fanned fears of a catastrophic economic collapse should golf courses and landscapers come up dry. For Thornton, the glass could be half full *and* half empty.

But he had best not find a blind salamander swimming in that glass. Thornton's rhetorical beef with what he sneeringly described as a "scrawny, underfed lizard" only intensified when

Bunton invoked the Endangered Species Act in its defense and ordered water restrictions. "It's time we draw a line in the sand to fight for consideration of humans and human rights," Thornton thundered. To place the needs of "this one little lizard" over those of millions of South Texans was "a perversion of what we should be trying to do in time of drought."

We had heard this complaint before. In 1994, Thornton's predecessor, Mayor Nelson Wolff, leveled similar charges against the Endangered Species Act during that year's water fracas and later appealed at a congressional hearing for relief from the act's allegedly onerous restrictions on human freedom. His testimony, along with that of other local and state officials nationwide, helped fuel the antienvironmental fervor Newt Gingrich and his minions capitalized on in the run-up to the 1994 congressional elections.

Taking a whack at salamanders had made for good politics in the past, and Mayor Thornton was not above grabbing a little electoral edge at the reptile's expense. That edge could cut both ways, as Gingrich was dismayed to discover when the Republican-dominated Congress tried to eliminate the Endangered Species Act and a host of other environmental regulations, only to suffer a monumental public relations beating. It turned out that informed voters understood that the much-maligned act, rather than being antihuman, was (and is) anthropocentric in its consequences: when it preserves the habitat for a salmon, a woodpecker, or a salamander, it also protects the water, air, and soil on which human life depends.

Judge Bunton understood how endangered South Texans

were, asserting in his controversial 1996 order that "the region's quality of life and economic future is imperiled" without a "fundamental change in the value the region places on fresh water." He urged changes that must include a "major effort to conserve and reuse Aquifer water, and implemented plans to import supplemental supplies of water." His reasoning was not dependent on the weather: it was as logical during episodes of crushing drought as it was in times of rushing rivers and lush lawns.

Indeed, the emergency Bunton described would not pass until San Antonians began paying the real costs associated with aquifer pumping and stopped being mesmerized by the miragelike claims that economic growth only flowed from plenty of cheap water. What seems inexpensive, after all, can prove quite costly. Keeping water prices low, observed political scientist Heywood Sanders, supports the fiction that people living in semiarid landscapes can create green suburbs "just like the Mid-West." Low-water costs free builders, who "need not pay for the development of water delivery systems," to construct subdivisions ever farther from the city's center. This pattern of dispersal persists only because, with the aquifer's availability, housing developers are free to "sink in their straws, and suck out water close to the source of consumption."

Industry's demands for water, especially among local computer-chip companies such as Sony and VLSI, testified as well to the hidden expenses associated with a cheap-water regime. Once touted as the means to local economic salvation, these tech corporations consumed such stunning quantities of water in their manufacturing processes that they threatened the financial boom they were supposed to generate. According to data compiled by the Southwest

Network for Environmental Justice and the Campaign for Responsible Technology, issued in the report *Sacred Waters: Life-Blood of Mother Earth*, the production of an average six-inch silicon wafer requires nearly 2,300 gallons of deionized water and discharges more than 2,800 gallons of wastewater. Those numbers add up quickly, and they point to a disturbing disparity: because industrial and commercial users of water pay less per 1,000 gallons of water consumed than do residences—and in some cases substantially less—homeowners help underwrite expansion of computer enterprises in this region. Austin was perhaps the first Texas city to discover that subsidizing the rapid development of its Silicon Hills proved a Faustian bargain.

Though San Antonio is not poised to become Austin South (or San Jose East), it has had its own devilish habits to break. Doing so has required a dramatic change in the pattern of water user fees and in the siting and construction of new homes, as well as important alterations in other aspects of regional work and life. These include, among others, a shift from spray to drip irrigation in agricultural production and a commensurate redesign of the landscape aesthetic, from greensward to xeriscape. Such water-thrifty choices may well be the key to the human future in this bioregion.

It is not that local elected officials were hesitant in the summer of 1996 to make a case coupling intense conservation with radical changes in water consumption. The once-a-week lawn watering ordinance, and the modest surcharge on households that pumped more than 17,205 gallons a month, had a visible impact. The suburban landscape went brown and cracks rippled through innumerable foundations as the dry land contracted. These attempts to control water usage, however worthy, were not enough. Major consumers were not targeted in meaningful ways. Estimates were that the top 10 percent of residential users gulped down 30 percent of the city's residential pumpage. Judge Bunton also charged that San Antonio's innumerable eighteen-hole golf courses absorbed up to 336 million gallons a month, "or as much as the total average for some 23,000 households." Although these enterprises had howled when the surcharge was enacted, their unquenchable thirst was not seriously curtailed.

That city politicos hesitated before cracking down on those whose influence matched their deep pockets was no surprise; they would have paid too heavy a price had they proposed a rigorous set of restrictions. This was also true in Austin and Uvalde. In San Antonio, however, term limits have compounded its leadership's reluctance to imagine, let alone argue for, environmentally sensitive, long-term solutions to its enduring water crisis.

In the early 1990s, when disgruntled citizens pushed through an ordinance stipulating that the city council and the mayor could only serve consecutive two-year terms, they believed they were liberating city hall. The idea was that we would gain better leadership and more committed management, a government of our own. The ensuing political inertia has revealed just how vain those hopes were. Without the possibility of a lengthy career in which public service and self-interest could be married, city council representatives have occupied a system of revolving chairs. Understandably, they have tried to slough off their responsibility for and leadership in the water debate. "Look, Henry Cisneros was the last mayor to seriously grapple with water issues," Sanders argued, "and even he couldn't pull it off." Mayor Thornton's actions in 1996 underscore this point. Only at the close of that summer's brutal hot spell did he publicly muse about the possible need for a future-oriented water strategy. His foxhole conversion, if such it was, suggested that when short-term gain alone defined the political stakes, that was what would drive politicians' calculations.

This political construct lay at the heart of the mayor's allegation that Judge Bunton had overstepped his bounds. In so arguing, Thornton admitted—albeit unconsciously—that San Antonio had been caught in a paralysis of its own making. Bunton acted because San Antonio would not. The paralysis nearly scuttled an initiative that was surely the bright spot in that summer of discontent. When the San Antonio Water System (SAWS), an agency governed by a city council–appointed board, mandated a surcharge on excess water consumption, the council nearly buckled under intense pressure from powerful opponents of the fee. That it stopped short of rescinding the measure had less to do with its support than with the recognition that the surcharge was scheduled to evaporate in September. The people's representatives had bought themselves time by doing nothing.

To develop a politics capable of proactive planning, the citizenry must scrap term limits, which, according to Sanders, "inhibit any serious capacity to plan for the community's future needs." One of those needs is to build a revitalized political culture that values sustained, energetic leadership; if established, that culture would allow local government to tackle the complicated issues that have long swirled around water policies. It would also allow this novelty: elected officials who govern with the community's long-term interests at heart.

In the short term, it is clear that SAWS, which has been on the cutting edge of local water conservation efforts, must continue to operate with a freedom the city council cannot yet replicate. SAWS cemented its reputation with its 1997 construction of a long overdue, but vital, network of pipes to distribute recycled water. For industrial consumption and recreational use—on those spongelike golf courses, for example—this "gray water" has decreased the drain on the aquifer by upward of 20 percent of current demand and has begun to distribute eleven billion gallons of recycled water a year. A tidy sum.

There is some irony in SAWS's laudable role as an active agent for conservation. Its potential for independent action kicked up a storm of protest in the spring of 1956, when voters went to the polls to determine whether to create a quasi-independent agency (the City Water Board) or to set up a city water department. The *San Antonio Light* spoke for many when it warned that an organization free of political oversight was a dangerous gamble; the newspaper likened its creation to playing "Stake in the Dark," a form of poker in which you wager without peeking at your cards. A much safer bet, it concluded, would be to put water policy in the hands of elected officials who would be responsive to the community's needs.

Voters thought otherwise, and an independent City Water Board was established. Had that not happened, an elected board responsive to a political environment renowned for its anti-environmentalism would have been the last set of hands in which to entrust the future of the metropolitan water agenda. Not forever will spring rains and summer showers rescue us; not for long will the frogs dance up a storm.

Running Dry

If, as a popular T-shirt asserts, "Golf Is Life," then there is a lot of living going on in the American Southwest. Climate is essential to understanding the vital link between the game and the region. Texas, New Mexico, and Arizona—the three principal southwestern states—benefit from an excess of 300 days of sunshine a year, which is conducive to year-round play. The salubrious weather is a particular incentive for those who live in more northerly and colder climes to head south and west for a winter round or three, just as it has encouraged the migration of millions of elderly Americans, many of whom have packed their clubs and followed the sun to retirement homes located in the Yuma desert, the Rocky Mountains, and the Rio Grande Valley. Whatever its purpose or destination, this travel has been financed by a surge in Americans' disposable income since the 1970s, which has underwritten the tremendous growth in the regional recreational and tourist infrastructure. This buildup has been nourished, too, by the vast, post–World War Two federal investment in the construction of an interlocking complex of dams, reservoirs, and water distribution systems throughout Arizona and New Mexico, and, to a lesser extent, Texas. Without ready access to water (and air conditioning), the region could not sustain the explosion of urban populations in Houston, Phoenix, Dallas, and San Antonio, which are now among the nation's ten largest cities.

Not all citizens of the Southwest drive, chip, and putt, but that is not due to any lack of fairways, bunkers, or greens. Capitalizing on the region's Sunbelt image, demographic transformation, and increased income levels, developers have built a staggering number of golf courses, most of which are tightly clustered around the fast-growing cities. Texas boasts almost 900, New Mexico claims 95, and Arizona another 351. Often laid out in high-end subdivisions, neatly tying together housing, recreation, and other luxe amenities, the well-watered courses have spawned a slew of secondary commercial activity. No wonder urban boosters tout the virtues of golf: the sport has expanded local service economies even as it has signaled the region's shift from its rural past into its suburban future. Founded in rain-swept, fifteenth-century eastern Scotland, golf has become the game of a dry twenty-first-century American Southwest.

No city takes this prospect more seriously than San Antonio. Home to forty-five golf courses, three of which are ranked in *Golf Digest*'s annual listing of the nation's 100 Greatest Courses, the South Texas metropolis is acclaimed as one of *Golf Magazine*'s Top 50 Worldwide Golfing Destinations. Such stellar designations are much prized for the visitors they lure to town; these guests' liberal spending habits have eased some of the economic pain brought on by a sharp decline in the Cold War–generated federal dollars that once streamed through the city's five major military bases. In San Antonio, tourism now pays the bills.

Little wonder that local business leaders, political mavens, and golf enthusiasts were delighted by the news in early 2001 that the Professional Golf Association of America (PGA) had teamed up with Lumberman's Investment Group of Austin to build a sprawling 2,800-acre resort amid the rolling hills of northern Bexar County. The promise of two new golf courses totaling thirty-six holes (with designs by golfing legend Jack Nicklaus) and a golf learning center, as well as an upscale 500-room hotel, ritzy shopping mall, and luxury housing, led Steve Moore, executive director of the Convention and Visitors Bureau, to enthuse: "The economic benefits are multifold. There would be the [public relations] and articles written about it and also an increased interest by leisure visitors and corporate and convention visitors." Even those who would potentially compete with the new courses shared Moore's faith that the PGA Village "would have a positive impact to position San Antonio as a golf destination." Courtney Connally, head pro at the Fair Oaks Ranch club, noted that the city was a natural for the proposed facility: "San Antonio really has a lot of attractions, the topography, the weather, and the family festivities." Those advantages, confirmed Jim Autry, PGA executive director, were what led his organization to select this site. San Antonio "is one of the top cities in America," he said. "You've got a wonderful town."

A conflicted city, too; as word spread about the new project, criticism exploded. At the core of the outrage was water. "How wonderful! A 36-hole golf course!" Patricia Coleman exclaimed in a letter to the *San Antonio Express-News*. "A 500-room hotel full of guests, all taking 30-minute showers. Fairway homes with lawns and gardens well above the price that the average citizen can afford, each with a minimum of 2½ baths, no doubt, and all over the Edwards Aquifer." Satire melted into anger when she pointed out that the region was entirely dependent on the aquifer for its potable water, and that it was afflicted with perennial, seasonal drought. Coleman was not alone when she prayed that "clearer heads will prevail when permits are sought for this ill-conceived pipe dream. We do not have the water to support this monstrosity."

In the succeeding months, local environmental groups analyzed the special taxing district the state legislature and city council created for the project, gauged PGA Village's political support, and investigated its potential to harm the aquifer's sensitive recharge features. Despite assurances that the large resort would install rigorous state-of-the-art environmental protections to ensure the maintenance of unsullied underground water, and that it would jump-start the urban economy with new work and tourist dollars, a coalition of activist organizations came together to challenge its construction. Two organizations with lengthy histories of grassroots protest in the city, Communities Organized for Public Services (COPS, founded in 1974) and METRO Alliance (founded in 1982), joined with the newly created SmartGrowth Coalition to launch a petition drive to overturn the city council's support for PGA Village. Their populist slogan—"It's Our

Money/It's Our Water"—bore electoral fruit: by July 2002, many more than the required 63,000 citizens had signed petitions, forcing a November 2002 special election. To dodge that inevitability, the city withdrew its proposal and worked with developers on another that would not have to come before the voters; the resort's target date for completion is 2006.

This struggle over water and growth in San Antonio may connect to a particular time and place, but it relates to millennial-old concerns about water use in this semiarid region. All those who have chosen to inhabit the San Antonio River valley have had to take into account the flow of water beneath and across the land. Whatever the form of settlement, and by whatever name the inhabitants have called themselves, each group, from the Tonkawa to the Spanish, the Mexicans to Americans, has framed its collective destiny and social structure around its capacity to draw upon available water supplies. It turns out that when early-twenty-first-century San Antonians fought over fairways, hotels, and housing, they were participating in an age-old drama.

Native American peoples had long exploited South Texas river valleys and creekbeds, where they had fished and harvested, foraged and hunted. Archeological evidence dug up along the tributaries of the San Antonio River reveals the presence of hunter-gatherers dating back more than 11,000 years. Those who inhabited these sites before the Spanish arrived, known collectively as the Tonkawa, searched for "live" water (which flowed during the hot summer months) by migrating along the arc of rivers that cut down through the Edwards Plateau. Their travels, from west to north, led them from the Nueces, Frio, and Medina

Rivers, to the San Antonio River, and on to the Guadalupe and Colorado Rivers, which run through present-day New Braunfels and Austin. As they roamed across this rough terrain, they made extensive use of the line of springs that bubbled up from the limestone bedrock.

But the Tonkawa never deemed it necessary to manipulate the regional waterscape to enhance food supplies. Unlike the Hohokum, who lived along the Salt River in what is now southern Arizona, they did not build channels through which to maneuver streamflow and irrigate crops—that is, they did not do so of their own accord. But by the late seventeenth and early eighteenth centuries, they at once chose and were compelled to give up their indigenous ways.

Spanish missionaries, pressing up from the south, brought with them diseases that decimated the indigenous population. At the missions the Spaniards established along the San Antonio River valley, many of the surviving Indians, often through forced conversion, were transformed into agricultural laborers.

The arrival of the Lipan Apache, who came to dominate the Edwards Plateau by 1700, also convinced some Tonkawa to take refuge in the recently established Spanish communities. No match for these invaders' military prowess, and seeking protection the Spanish seemed to provide, Tonkawa and other displaced Indian peoples converted to Catholicism, a Spanish prelate declared, "for fear of the Apache." His insight suggests that a broader transformation was under way: "By the end of the 17th century," argues archaeologist T. N. Campbell, "the Indians of southern Texas were already beginning to face what most hunting and gathering peoples of the world have had to face," including "population decline, territorial displacement, segregation and ideological pressure, loss of ethnic identity, and absorption by invading armies."

This fundamental alteration is most visible in the work the Tonkawa took up under the Spanish flag—their indispensable, backbreaking efforts to dig acequias, or irrigation ditches. With crowbars, picks, and axes, they cut trenches that ran parallel to the San Antonio River, from its headwaters downstream to the missions. This distribution system transformed soil that had never been cultivated into arable land and provided water to a small but permanent population consisting of civilians, Indians, missionaries, and soldiers. By capturing their converts' energy, the Spanish had harnessed the river's flow. Their control over land and labor freed them to introduce a new stage of human economy to the region: agriculture and ranching. With water came power.

Also, with water came growth. That is what Capt. Domingo Ramón predicted in 1716, when his expedition to eastern Texas briefly sojourned in the San Antonio valley. Like others before and after him, he was struck by the area's river-fed verdancy, the luxuriance of its surrounding "nopals, poplars, elms, grapevines, black mulberry trees, laurels, strawberry vines, and genuine fan palms." This arboreal beauty also signified town-building potential. After examining the first of the gushing springs he would encounter, Ramón concluded that there "was sufficient water here for a city of one-quarter league," an estimate he no doubt expanded when he traversed the nearby San Antonio River. The subsequent Spanish settlement, with its substantial investment in acequias to enhance agricultural, commercial, and household consumption, was predicated on Ramón's insight into the essential connection between streamflow and urban development, for without a ready and consistent access to water, there could be no San Antonio de Béxar.

So Mexicans and Americans would conclude as well. Indeed, neither of the two successors to the former Spanish territory in South Texas was able immediately to alter the degree to which water, its presence and absence, conditioned life in this frontier outpost. Each new government—the Mexicans took over in the early 1820s, the Americans in the mid-1840s—made full use of the acequias to distribute water to the citizenry; each patterned its regulatory authority over water on Spanish legal precedents. That each group was able to exist within this older system was a consequence of San Antonio's distance from major population centers and markets; it grew very slowly until after the Civil War and was therefore able to absorb increases in demand.

Even when the delivery system was stressed, the community generally finessed dry spells with a conservative use of water. Its need to adapt to this environmental pressure puzzled poet Sidney Lanier, who spent the month of February 1873 in San Antonio, then a modest town of 12,000. Among the town's peculiarities, he wrote, was that "it was built along the banks of two limpid streams, yet it drinks rain-water collected in cisterns." Had he remained in town for the later dry months, he would have better understood why the citizenry was compelled to harvest rainfall.

A mere four years later, even rigorous conservation could not stave off a looming, perilous decrease of potable water supplies.

The locus of change was the 1877 arrival of the first railroad—the Galveston, Harrisburg, and San Antonio; the growth it sparked would overwhelm the acequia water-delivery system. This untenable situation was made worse by a lack of sewers, such that commercial effluent was dumped into the ditches or slopped into the river or creeks. Liquid household wastes and human excreta meant to be captured in cesspools or underground privy vaults invariably leached into the soil and nearby wells. The resultant public health problems were expected to get worse as the city swelled in size: "The primitive means of . . . disposal answered while [San Antonio] was a village," the head of the West Texas Medical Association noted, but "such is inadequate to a population of 30,000, and cannot continue without disastrous effects." Not until the mid-1890s, after years of political debate, did a city-wide sewage system go on line.

However innovative, this welcome change in urban sanitation disposal depended on an even more radical alteration in water supply and delivery, which transformed the historic relationship between the people and the land. Once compelled to live under severe environmental constraints, San Antonians of the 1890s entered an era in which technology seemed to promise a release from nature.

The key promoter of this brave new world was George W. Brackenridge. A shrewd and contentious man, he was the city's major banker, publisher of the *Daily Express*, and lead shareholder of the privately owned Water Works Company. It did not hurt that he owned hundreds of acres surrounding the springs the San Antonio River rushed from, and it was from this property that his company captured and distributed its flow. By 1885, Brackenridge had invested in pumps to push water through what grew to be 100 miles of pipeline serving residential and commercial customers; the successful entrepreneur even rented a fire hydrant network to the city, to the tune of $25,000 a year. His dominance of public works and the civic economy was controversial, leading rival newspapers to denounce him as "the Monopolist" and politicians— especially in election season—to lambaste his imperial grip.

The community had only itself to blame. Its legendary aversion to levying taxes to pay for infrastructure, its frequent loan defaults, and its curious refusal to pay its bills meant that private investment was essential to the creation of city services. Even when Brackenridge offered to sell the waterworks to the city at bargain prices, the political leadership rejected the deals. They may have feared and despised him, but they also depended on his financial acumen and considerable assets.

Brackenridge drew on those ample resources again in the early 1890s, when, urged on by a medical official who was convinced that artesian wells would provide pure water and inoculate the citizenry from cholera and other infectious diseases, he began to drill test wells near *ojo de aqua*, the source of the San Antonio River. A 3,000-foot well came up empty. But in 1893 he struck pay dirt downtown, leading the *Daily Express* to exclaim: "The fresh water supply of San Antonio is apparently unlimited. It has been increased three million gallons for each twenty-four hours by a splendid strike . . . on the property of Colonel George Bracken-ridge on Market Street." Additional wells, and the purchase of steam-driven pumps to flush water along what one historian has called the "mushrooming tendrils" of the Water Works Company pipelines, ensured the year-round availability of clean and cheap water to a city long accustomed to episodic drought.

Readily tapped and distributed, the new water supplies nourished the rapid population growth that defined San Antonio's twentieth-century history and its corresponding economic expansion. By 1925, when the city finally scraped together $7 million to buy the private waterworks, renaming it the City Water Board, San Antonio boasted nearly 200,000 inhabitants, making it the largest city in Texas.

This boisterous pattern of growth came with a series of environmental costs and social concerns. As early as 1897, Brackenridge acknowledged to the *San Antonio Express* that "his steady pumping of the wells" was lowering the level of the Edwards Aquifer, diminishing the natural flow from the community's many springs, reducing the volume of the San Antonio River and San Pedro Creek, and elevating anxieties about the long-term availability of local water supplies. He even admitted that "in the course of time it will be advisable for the city to exercise the higher right that the government had over individuals to the extent of controlling the boring of new artesian wells," but he could not accept that the river would run dry. He, like subsequent generations of San Antonians, wanted very much to believe that "the great underground reservoir from which the river flows will be replenished and the stage of water will become normal again."

The water table and streamflow never returned to the levels of the prepumping era. These were not the only water-related problems the city faced in the twentieth century. Although the distribution of potable water would become publicly owned, it was not equitably distributed until the 1970s. The city's poor rarely had indoor plumbing and often had to trek blocks to locate outdoor faucets. Explosive population increases in the post–World War Two era, combined with a crippling drought in the 1950s, intensified these inequities and reminded the city how powerful nature could be in shaping the contours of life in South Texas.

But cracks in foundations, buckled water mains, and the occasionally empty spigot did not halt the city's automobile-driven, northerly sprawl of housing subdivisions, shopping malls, and commercial nodes. By the 1970s, some developments even threatened to seal over the aquifer's recharge zones. This situation was doubly alarming, for the Edwards remained the sole source of potable water. In the 1950s, penny-pinching politicians and a frugal water board had discovered that their search for more water was hobbled by the city's paltry financial resources. This situation held true until the 1990s, such that the community's unending struggle over issues of water quality and quantity is best depicted each summer in the ominous graphs that illustrate daily fluctuations in the aquifer's level. San Antonio's diet of cheap water turned out to be an expensive, nerve-racking habit.

Since the 1970s, protesters have challenged the city council's relentless pursuit of growth for its own sake; giving pause as well has been federal enforcement of the Endangered Species Act to protect flora and fauna living within the aquifer and its springs. By the 1990s, it seemed clear that the era of unrestrained pumping was ending, just as the city experienced yet another surge in population, yet another damaging dry spell, and yet another set of sky-high summer temperatures. The result was a long-overdue reassessment of the city's water policies, the central goal of which became the hunt for new water sources to decrease reliance on the aquifer.

The proposed first step was to build a reservoir in southern Bexar County, impounding the Medina River. Originally discussed in the early 1950s, and shelved when engineering studies suggested the site's inadequacies, the idea for the so-called Applewhite Reservoir was revived in the early 1990s. Forced onto the ballot through a successful, antireservoir petition drive, the surface-water project was rejected at the polls in 1991 and again in 1994. For this second round, anti-Applewhite forces rallied under the banner "No Means No!" and successfully raised doubts about the reservoir's projected costs, environmental impacts, and hydrological integrity.

The city's hunt for water subsequently shifted away from schemes that might face electoral scrutiny to a strategy that would finesse the political process yet develop mechanisms to slake the city's deep thirst. The city realized that by increasing water costs it could generate sufficient revenue to fund initiatives to conserve present-day resources and tap additional supplies. The driving force behind what has emerged as the city's latest phase in water politics has been the San Antonio Water System (SAWS). Born of the old City Water Board, by way of Brackenridge's original Water Works Company, SAWS in late September 2000 halted the cheap-water era its organizational progenitors had sustained since the late nineteenth century. The agency's board agreed to levy a monthly water supply fee that would boost bills by nearly 21 percent (with additional hikes scheduled); set "a conservation-

oriented pricing structure for the utility's general class [of con-
sumers]—apartments, businesses and industry"; equalize water
rates among the different classes of users; and establish a bill-
assistance program to ensure that low-income households would
not be adversely affected by rising costs. As critics were quick to
point out, the proposed structure actually lowered per-unit prices
for large commercial users, but overall the new approach was to
net SAWS an additional $20 million in its first year and ever more
thereafter. "While we have not come to the perfect conclusion,"
then-Mayor Howard Peak admitted, "the balance is pretty good
and is a significant next step for us in the process of refining our
rates and providing money necessary to buy new water for San
Antonio."

Actually, the initial move was to squeeze new water out of old.
SAWS, beginning in the late 1990s, rolled out an innovative water
recycling program. Treated, nonpotable wastewater is now piped
throughout San Antonio for large-ground landscaping, including
golf courses, office parks, and commercial and educational sites.
By late 2001, SAWS declared that it was recycling approximately
11 billion gallons a year. This news dovetailed with a massive push
to educate consumers about the need to be conservation minded,
which entailed financial incentives to shift to more water-efficient
plumbing. The impact has been striking: since the mid-1980s,
water use has dropped 32 percent, with a 45 percent decline predicted by 2015. San Antonio's per capita consumption, once
among the highest in the state, is now the lowest. Conservation
proved its worth, observed SAWS board president James Mayor,
"because [it] is the cheapest source of new water available to us."

That did not stop SAWS from pursuing more costly supplies. Like other public and private purveyors throughout the Southwest, it aggressively entered water markets, using its capital to sop up unused rights in Bexar and its surrounding counties. It also successfully negotiated with an ALCOA lignite mine in Bastrop County, northeast of Austin, for 90,000 acre-feet of water in the Simsboro Aquifer, a basin transfer that received the legislature's blessing. South of San Antonio, SAWS began to purchase tracts of land over the sandy Carrizo-Wilcox Aquifer so that it could store excess Edwards flow in what amounts to a modern-day underground cistern. The total tab for the project, which includes a new water treatment plant, wells, and pipeline infrastructure, will top $215 million, a huge investment and second only to that paid out for a similar facility by cash-rich, but very arid Las Vegas, Nevada. For a community that had so rarely invested in its future, San Antonio seemed to have undergone a personality change with the ringing in of the new millennium.

Not everything changed. Local water fights did not cease; they simply changed venue. As individual farmers and ranchers reaped a profit by selling portions of their water rights to SAWS, their rural communities worried about the decline in traditional agrarian values. San Antonio's reach across watersheds to divert water to the city has provoked protests against its practice of water imperialism. Closer to home, the decrease in the city's dependence on the aquifer has generated some worry that the newfound independence perversely will accelerate construction over the Edwards: why protect it if its waters are no longer so essential?

Embedded in these and other plaintive appeals is a core concern: South Texas, like the rest of the Southwest, has not yet devised a common language to discuss water, nor to define past uses, articulate contemporary needs, or plot future demand. Perhaps it is impossible to think about water as a commons and to act accordingly. But like others living in the fast-growing region, San Antonians have discovered that the lack of such binding language and unifying vision has impeded the resolution of a tangle of economic, environmental, and social needs. Making this case abundantly clear was the divisive debate that erupted over plans to build the PGA Village complex over one of the most sensitive portions of the Edwards Aquifer recharge zone.

CONSTRUCTION ZONE

Neighborhood Watch

McCullough Avenue runs north-south between downtown San Antonio and the interior suburbs that lie within Loop 410. It is a vague sort of arterial roadway; sometimes its contains two lanes, sometimes four—an uncertainty that adds to its charm even as it heightens automotive anxiety. It nonetheless offers a less congested means by which to navigate the city's north-central corridor than does McAllister Freeway (u.s. 281), an elevated slab of concrete that parallels it to the east. That is why many of my Olmos Park neighbors who work downtown prefer McCullough's rolling blacktop, and the ash, oak, and pecan trees that shade its edge, to the expressway's sharp curves and jammed lanes. Driving on it might be an adventure, a friend acknowledged, "but at least I feel grounded."

The avenue is grounded in another sense: along its run out of town it exposes some of the rough edges of contemporary metropolitan life. This is particularly evident as McCullough rises out of the central core and into the elevated terrain of Tobin Hill, site of the city's first streetcar suburbs. Much of its late-nineteenth-century housing stock has either fallen into disarray or to the wrecking ball. These tottering structures and overgrown lots, scattered amid a now faceless built landscape, make a mockery of what was once touted as urban renewal.

Less visible, but no less significant, is the division McCullough delineates between zones of intense affluence and poverty. As the avenue crests the hills, passes through the Monte Vista historic district—another former streetcar suburb—and crosses Hildebrand Avenue, once the city's northern limits, it cuts between Olmos Park on the east and Kenwood on the west. These neighborhoods' status and standing could not be more disparate, probably the greatest in the city.

Incorporated in the 1920s, and one of the city's first automobile suburbs, Olmos Park has long been perceived as an elite enclave. The perception is sustained by its substantial dwellings, tree-lined streets, and robust average household income. Kenwood, home to many of the Hispanic and African American servants who worked in the nearby manses of Olmos Park, remains among the poorest of districts. Its oldest abodes are of the infamous shotgun variety, their slight wooden frames stacked on cinder-block foundations. Until the 1960s, Kenwood lacked running water and utilities, and its continued destitution is captured in this grim statistic from the late 1990s: one-third of its population then lived on less than $15,000 a year.

These stunning disparities in wealth and shelter are reinforced in educational prospects. Those children who live west of McCullough attend schools in the San Antonio Independent

School District. Edison High School serves this area, and its student body is more than 92 percent Hispanic; only three-quarters of the school's students graduate. Youth living east of McCullough go to Alamo Heights Independent School District; its high school's population is 70 percent white, and 96 percent of its senior class heads off to college.

Giving physical form to these layers of divergence is the odd streetscape. On McCullough's western edge is a jumbled commercial corridor: furniture and plumbing supply shops, a hardware store, a car wash, auto repair shops, a gas station, and veterinary clinics jostle for drivers' attention and wall off Kenwood from their sight. On the east is a soft border of green lawn, tree cover, and limestone residences. Even the feeder streets from the two neighborhoods are distinct. On each side of McCullough, streets bear different names and do not line up—Stanford is staggered off from Dora; Mandalay does not connect with Zilla; and Hermosa misses Joy.

But then there is little reason to navigate between the two neighborhoods. Indeed, these social divisions and spatial distinctions were a deliberate consequence of Olmos Park's design, which segregated it from Kenwood and, by extension, the wider city. Yet its residents' desire for isolation and difference were never fully realized, as the community's development has been bound up with and illustrative of the political tensions and social problems that dominated San Antonio—and the nation—in the first decades of the twentieth century.

Herman Charles Thorman, the initial developer of Olmos Park, was something of a Horatio Alger figure. He was raised in rural northwestern Ohio and arrived in San Antonio in 1909 with great ambition but little capital. Yet he managed to invest wisely in a Texas oil venture, the proceeds of which allowed him to speculate in San Antonio real estate. By the mid-1920s he had built middle-class subdivisions in Highlands to the south of downtown, and along Fredericksburg Road northwest of the central core; he was also responsible for Country Club Estates, cottage homes bordering the San Antonio Country Club, which lay in the north-central sector of town. By 1925, Thorman had constructed an estimated 1,200 homes, a substantial number at a time when most suburban housing development in the United States was on a much smaller scale.

Thorman's success was only partly due to individual initiative. He capitalized on the city's preexisting radial pattern of growth, which the streetcars and railroads established in the late nineteenth and early twentieth centuries, and which the automobile quickly extended. His developments on Fredericksburg Road and in the Highlands district are prime examples of the kind of suburb the automobile made possible.

So, too, with Olmos Park. Its location on the northern edge of San Antonio enabled Thorman to exploit one of the most significant public works projects in the city's history—the construction of the Olmos Dam. For all its impact on flood control, the dam had far-reaching economic consequences as well. As the *San Antonio Express* understood, it quickly "stabilized property values throughout the city, and has given San Antonio a new standing among large investors of capital." Its impact on peripheral residential development was just as great. Thorman understood that the road atop the dam would serve as a vital bridge across the often dangerous Olmos Creek and would offer "a new crosstown thoroughfare linking Alamo Heights on the east with Laurel Heights on the west." Because his property was situated between these two locations, it would benefit from new traffic patterns along the city's north side and make accessible (and profitable) his as-yet undeveloped piece of land.

Prior to the dam's construction, Thorman declared in an interview, "no facilities existed for some considerable distance for crossing between the east and west divisions on the north of greater San Antonio." This meant that residential development in metropolitan San Antonio had "spread out to the north from downtown something after the manner of a fan." The dam changed that outward thrust, Thorman concluded, by "encouraging the filling in with residential development of some considerable proportion of the underdeveloped territory within the fan." It is clear, from a newspaper advertisement focusing on the dam as a highway, that the Olmos Dam and the automobile were integral to the creation of Olmos Park: in the advertisement, which Thorman paid for, a rush of cars speeds across the dam from Alamo Heights toward a banner emblazoned with the words "Park Hills Estates," one of early the names given to Thorman's proposed subdivision.

The automobile was also responsible for the community's physical form. Rather than reproduce the gridiron pattern characterizing most of San Antonio, a pattern that obliterated the natural contours of the land for the sake of convenience and efficiency, Thorman designed Olmos Park to control the car and provide a sharp break—visual and physical—from the surrounding grid. After giving "careful thought to the planning of these Estates [such] that the great natural beauty and splendid position of this property would be enhanced," he embraced what he called the "parkway system of development." Drawing on the landscape practices of the legendary Frederick Law Olmsted and Kansas City developer J. C. Nichols, he laid down broad avenues and drives that wind among the native oak trees and roll gently over the hills.

An array of natural and man-made barriers insulated the new community. To its east and north lay the Olmos Creek flood basin, land forever uninhabitable with the building of the dam; in the future portions of that basin would be used for a city park. To the south lay a quarry (in which Trinity University would later be located), and on its western edge ran the Missouri Pacific rail lines. Each of these helped prevent the encroachment of undesirable development and, when combined with the centripetal force that the "parkway system" exerted on movement in the community's interior, set Olmos Park apart from the surrounding environs. It "was really a little town on the edge of a big town and was situated where it was 'out of the way,'" one longtime resident of Olmos Park wrote, "and because of the street layout, nobody went thru it or even came into it except us."

Intensifying its social exclusivity were the legal codes governing the lives and affairs of those who moved into the suburb. Along with other upper-class suburbs developed in early-twentieth-century America—Houston's River Oaks, the Country Club District of Kansas City, and Baltimore's Roland Park—Olmos Park adopted a restrictive covenant to perpetuate racial segregation and maintain property values. The covenant made it clear that Olmos Park was for whites only: no portion of the property could be "sold, conveyed or leased to any person who is not of the caucasian race." Any violation of this stipulation was punishable by law and would "work as a forfeiture of the title to the particular subdivision of property," a clear signal that the community's right to racial segregation superseded the rights of the individual property owner. The covenant applied across time, as well, and was made "running with the land" and bound upon "the grantee, his heirs, devisees, executors, administrators, successors or assigns." The restrictions, Thorman assured buyers, would "forever stand good."

With restrictions that were, in the builder's words, "sensibly designed to protect your home and every home from the encroachments of inferiority," Olmos Park's covenant was arguably the most rigorous in San Antonio. The required lot sizes were larger, minimum costs were higher, and prices per front-foot were steeper, creating the kind of expansive "grounds that are demanded by those families who build fine homes." These elevated prices, and the substantial lawns they produced, made it difficult for any but a select few to buy into the community.

Among those who called it home, wrote Green Peyton, a novelist and journalist, in *San Antonio: City in the Sun* (1946), were "rich oilmen and cattle ranchers." But not, he mused, "many sheep and goat men. . . . They do not have the social pretensions of the old cattle families," preferring to "congregate in the garish lobby of the Gunter Hotel, in shirtsleeves, still wearing their ranch hats and boots."

This anecdotal evidence of the social standing of those who

bought homes in Olmos Park is underscored in data emerging from the San Antonio City Directory. The new development attracted a growing group of San Antonio's wealthy commercial and business elite who hitherto had lived in areas threatened by the expansion of the downtown commercial sector or lacking such restrictive covenants. Its cachet was also tied to its automotive character and therefore signaled the decline of the older streetcar-based subdivisions. Among some of Olmos Park's earliest residents was Britain R. Webb, who moved there from West French Place on Tobin Hill; a vice president of the City Central Bank and Trust and regional manager for the Buick Motor Company, Webb illustrated the emerging new economy in south-central Texas. Joining him were a clutch of others involved in the burgeoning automotive business, including Raymond Woodward, owner of Morgan-Woodward, a local Ford dealership; Joseph Edwards, an auditor for the city's Packard distributor; Clarence Gardner, treasurer of the Mountjoy Parts Company, which specialized in automobile engines; and J. Benjamin Robertson of the Luthy Battery Equipment Company.

Other entrepreneurs erected homes along Olmos Park's quiet streets, among them Carl D. Newton, another executive at City Central Bank and Trust Company, who owned Fox Photo, the local Kodak outlet. George Piper was a manager at the downtown Stowers Furniture Company, Morris Richbook and Charles Eidelberg operated Richbook's Department Store, and Alfred Beyer owned a local appliance company and a string of parking lots. One final group attracted to Olmos Park closely resembled H. C. Thorman himself in terms of economic success and business interests. Henry Catto made his fortune in oil and later established a major insurance company, and Urban Wagner headed the Kelwood Company, a building and contracting firm, and shared an interest in urban development with R. Thomas McDermott, who headed real estate and construction concerns.

Benefiting from San Antonio's development as a market center for a large South Texas hinterland, these men and their families were attracted to the exclusivity Olmos Park afforded, and by the chance to avoid city taxes and escape direct participation in city governmental and political affairs. Until the late 1930s it was possible to maintain this isolationist posture toward the larger community because it meshed with the then-dominant city machine's interests.

Like other urban machines in American cities in the early twentieth century, San Antonio's politicians were able to bargain over a largely controllable electorate. While the votes of east side blacks and west side Hispanics often required a direct financial investment, these votes were a known (and purchasable) commodity. The middle-class Anglo residents of the growing suburban tracts to the north were far less predictable; they often voted against machine candidates and the bond issues they supported, believing that the monies the bonds generated were used to cement an ever-tighter relationship between the machine and its working-class supporters. They weren't wrong: politicians everywhere have built parks, erected police substations, and repaired streets to curry allegiance. But because white northsiders generally rejected this working relationship, the city politicos did not target their neighborhoods for annexation (why bring in voters who might challenge your power?). Instead, local politicos did something curious: they provided water lines and police protection to Olmos Park free of charge. Apparently they were willing to provide these benefits, knowing they would not have to face the potential political complications posed by a neighborhood filled with upper-income and reform-minded voters. Olmos Park and other north side subdivisions were thus able to maintain the image of independence from the city while accepting its services.

Olmos Park was not forever insulated from the political forces that roiled metropolitan politics. By the late 1930s, its casual form of self-governance and its informal working relationship with the city came under assault—a result of the national reform agenda embodied in Franklin Roosevelt's New Deal and local insurgent politics. When that happened, the community immediately sought to incorporate, a move that the City of San Antonio would vigorously contest.

The massive federal aid emanating from Washington in the mid-1930s brought considerable civic investment to San Antonio, including the improvement and beautification of what is now the Riverwalk, the paving and improvement of streets, and the construction of a new post office, the city zoo, and Alamo Stadium. Local reformers also began to agitate to bring an end to machine rule. The infusion of federal aid and the emergence of an active reform movement in San Antonio were interconnected. The federal dollars served as patronage to bolster the political standing of the reformers, whose efforts received an additional boost. In 1938–39 Mayor C. K. Quin became the focus of a series of investigations and, later, of indictments over the temporary hiring of new city workers, a swelling of the payroll that just happened to coincide with the date of the Democratic primary election. In the spring of 1939, Maury Maverick, a former congressman and staunch New Dealer, led an effort to oust Quin in the May city election.

Running for mayor on what he called the "Fusion Ticket," Maverick entered a race crowded with four other slates, each of which claimed to be the most good-government-oriented alternative. The platform of Maverick's Fusion group called for elimination of the Quin machine and the eventual change from a commission form of government to a city-manager system. Maverick also called for lower taxes, a moderate increase in city hiring, and a more efficient delivery of urban services. But his image as a New Dealer and charges that he was a leftist dogged his campaign; fueling these charges was his promise to construct a number of expensive physical improvement projects, such as parks on the "colored" east side, that New Deal revenues would fund. Maverick represented a threat to the venerable city machine and to the customary way of doing governmental business in San Antonio.

Nonetheless, on May 9, 1939, Maverick and most of his Fusion Ticket captured city hall. His campaign and political triumph—a watershed in city politics—also had an immediate impact on tiny Olmos Park. On the day of Maverick's victory, local attorney Albert Negley filed an incorporation petition for Olmos Park with the Bexar County commissioners' court. One newspaper quoted Negley as arguing that "the desire of the persons living in the area to be united" was the reason for seeking municipal status, a desire accelerated by fears that the new mayor might seek to annex the community to increase the city's wealth and tax base.

The petition was the first step in Olmos Park's rapid incorporation effort. On May 23, its 1,550 residents voted overwhelmingly in support of incorporation, 237 to 6. Developer H. C. Thorman, a resident of Olmos Park, not only endorsed the community's new status as an independent polity but agreed to hold the incorporation election in the rear of his real estate office.

This incorporation effort followed by about two weeks a similar successful effort in nearby Terrell Hills. And together they set off a spate of incorporation attempts in neighboring subdivisions on San Antonio's north side. The fear of city annexation was widespread, and concern over the lax policies of city service delivery was well founded. Less than two months after the election of Maverick's Fusion Ticket, its members were pressing for a radical change in the provision of fire and police services. Fire and Police Commissioner Louis Lipscomb threatened to end protection of the incorporated suburbs unless they made some arrangements to cover the costs of service. Mayor Maverick declared that "the city of San Antonio would no longer carry the burdens for these areas beyond the city limit." His efforts proved less than successful. While he headed off other attempted incorporations, Olmos Park maintained its political independence and even managed to secure fire protection through a contractual arrangement with the city.

In this, Olmos Park's incorporation varied substantially from the model of suburban polities providing special or unique public services. Unlike Beverly Hills, California, or Dallas's Highland

Park, which incorporated as a part of their developmental strategies, and which also enjoyed full-fledged self-governance, Olmos
Park incorporated well after its construction. Even after it had
incorporated, its elected officers served without salary and the city
itself did not impose a tax or directly raise revenue. This lack of
governmental activity would encourage another reform mayor,
Gus Mauerman, to seek to annex the suburb in 1945. He too
would fail in the last serious attempt to absorb Olmos Park into
San Antonio proper.

Even if Mauerman or Maverick had succeeded, however,
theirs would have been a partial victory. That's because Olmos
Park's independent political status is not the most important force
defining its communal life. What is? Ask any contemporary real
estate agent, and she will confirm that the source of the community's cohesion is the schools its children attend. Founded in the
mid-1920s, Alamo Heights Independent School District serves
the sister suburbs of Alamo Heights, Terrell Hills, and Olmos
Park. That Olmos Park kids ride yellow buses bound for AHISD
schools to their east, and do not travel west across McCullough
Avenue to classrooms in which Kenwood children study, rein-
forces the enclave's high property values, political orientation, and
social homogeneity. The bus route also underscores the community's considerable disconnection from the poorer neighborhood
and school district to its west. Put another way, the school district
boundary line that runs along McCullough, however invisible, is
every bit as directive as the center stripe that regulates the avenue's
daily flow of traffic.

Edifice Complex

In Heaven, the talk had been about Henry Cisneros. (That's "Heaven" the hair salon, where, if you call and the receptionist is busy, she'll deadpan, "Heaven, will you hold?" Happily.) The conversation that day had centered on the phoenixlike resurgence of San Antonio's fallen angel, the city's first Hispanic mayor in the modern era, whose fast-track career had been derailed in 1989 by confessions of adultery. That four years later he had climbed back into the limelight, and had garnered considerable notice as President Clinton's secretary of the U.S. Department of Housing and Urban Development, did not surprise the stylists at Heaven: what else would you expect from the man one of them called the "Aztec God"?

Part of Cisneros's resurrection was attributed to the very large house this god had built—at the taxpayers' expense. A dome, actually—the Alamodome, as it is tagged—which opened in May 1994 to much fanfare. The local media, which for years had suppressed information about Cisneros's love life, devoted front-page coverage to and published special pull-out sections of the grand event. In print large and small, they detailed Cisneros's political efforts to secure voter approval for the stadium and praised the social vision that led to the vast complex's development. The *Wall Street Journal* and other national and regional organs swelled the chorus, pumping up the building and the man to great heights. To judge from the media cheers, "Mr. Alamodome," as Cisneros came to be known, had proved correct when, during the campaign in late 1988 and early 1989 to secure the citizens' approval, he vowed that the building's opening would mark the River City's "Year of Emergence."

What that claim meant was never clear or therefore particularly persuasive. The dome was heralded as the means to financial security for this impoverished community. As mayor, Cisneros promised that the facility would correct San Antonio's chronic poverty, low tax base, and undereducated populace. In the run-up to the 1989 vote, for example, he championed its capacity to lure convention business, draw national sporting events, if not a National Football League franchise, and serve as a magnet for tourism—all of which would expand the city's workforce and generate a more sustained economic growth. Dreamed up in the midst of the deep recession of the mid-1980s, which was brought on by the collapse of the local real estate market and the self-destruction of the statewide banking industry, the dome project promised a tantalizing quick fix.

The belief that the construction of a single building—however large—could reverse a declining regional economy was absurd, though it was typical of the national development talk of

American mayors. And this was not the first time during his term that Cisneros had made such an audacious claim about the impact of public funding on the local economy. Earlier he had secured federal monies to construct what was billed as Fiesta Plaza, a bright pink stucco retail mall plopped down west of the downtown core and, more significantly, just west of one of its feeder highways, Interstate 10. This large shopping center, he promised, would provide a renaissance for the economically depressed, largely Hispanic west side. Alas, it offered no such relief: Fiesta Plaza closed its doors shortly after they opened. The center was a victim of bad siting, mismanagement, and unrealistic expectations. For years this pink elephant, with its boarded-up windows, stood as an unsettling reminder of Cisneros's failed urban vision. How appropriate that the ghastly eyesore would later fall beneath the bulldozer's blade (and, in the late 1990s, would serve as the site of a downtown campus of the University of Texas at San Antonio).

The Alamodome has not suffered a similar fate, though its critics have renamed it the Alamodoom. Still, this triumph of Cisneros's redevelopment ambitions did not bring about the economic windfall it was projected to produce. Nor has it fulfilled its planners' euphoric dreams. They insisted, for example, that because the facility would open almost debt-free, something no other domed stadium in the nation could claim, its chances of success were excellent. But success in what sense? Jobs, they said. Once the construction work was completed, however, some of the most highly skilled, and thus highly paid, labor associated with the building drifted away. A series of equally temporary, if low-skilled, low-wage jobs typically associated with sports arenas and convention centers replaced the skilled construction jobs. And even these meager-paying positions were jeopardized in the fall of 2002 when the dome's main tenant, the NBA San Antonio Spurs, furled their championship banners and moved into their gleaming new arena, the SBC Center, far to the northeast of downtown. Their departure, driven by the team's desire to maximize its profit in a smaller, more basketball-friendly arena, has undercut the dome's ability to generate a sustained cash flow for the city. Although in direct competition with the dome, the SBC Center is much like that bigger space in terms of how the voters of Bexar County were persuaded to tax themselves for its construction. Once again, the commercial economic benefits of a new arena were stressed; once more, sports and entertainment were touted as an economic elixir. And you can be certain that in ten to fifteen years, when yet another large sports complex is brought before the public, these same arguments will be employed. We have not learned that poverty cannot be diminished nor economies resuscitated if the citizenry is relegated to hawking beer, parking cars, or flipping burgers.

That was what local activist Father Rosendo Urrabazo had in mind when he told a *Wall Street Journal* reporter in 1994 that "public money should be used for public good," a critique of the Alamodome's social impact that was buried in the last paragraph of that newspaper's lengthy, celebratory article about the dome's opening. He had a point: the dome has not served the broader public good—even in the rather narrow terms its backers employed. Its cavernous space has lured few large conventions to

town and failed therefore to boost tourist spending. No NFL
franchise has seriously considered moving to the Alamo City,
either. For all its size, the dome lacks the amenities and crowd
capacity that premiere stadia must boast. More detrimental is the
city's level of poverty and its small television market, among other
economic factors, all of which are not attractive to prospective
owners who must generate a substantial stream of income to
ensure success. San Antonio, with the exception of the Spurs, is a
minor-league city.

Much more to the liking of the dome's supporters was the
boilerplate boosterism attributed to Henry Cisneros, which is
inscribed on a massive, aluminum panel bolted above an aisle
leading to the dome's interior: "Over its life may this building help
many millions of us share the joys of coming together in faith, in
prosperity, and in the celebration of our common purposes."

Housing Project

During a punishing cold snap in mid-January 1997, just days before Henry Cisneros left his job as secretary of HUD for the bright lights of Univision, the Los Angeles–based, U.S. Spanish-language television network, Serefino Castillo crouched over a metal washtub, the only source of heat for the dilapidated, tin-roofed shack he rented on Monterey Street on San Antonio's near-west side.

As temperatures dropped below freezing on the evening of January 14, the 89-year-old man tossed a stack of wood into the basin, set it afire, and then hauled the crude portable heater into his abode. His was a well-tested technique: Castillo's neighbors later agreed that he had regularly employed this makeshift fireplace during that winter's unusually numbing weather.

Those life-giving embers would also be responsible for Castillo's death. At some point during the early morning, sparks shot out of the washtub, igniting a fire that gutted his home. Whether the flames or fumes ultimately killed him was not clear, and, to judge from the intense media coverage of the event, it did not really matter precisely how he died. What mattered was that he had lived in such ramshackle conditions, surrounded by twelve equally tumbledown units, without heat or other basic utilities, the whole sharing one outdoor toilet. Embarrassed, the city moved swiftly to condemn, then tear down, many of the eyesores, only to catch flak for evicting the impoverished tenants in the midst of a cold snap. "We're not in the business of throwing people out in the street," then–City Councilman Juan Solis told the *San Antonio Express-News*, but "this decision is for their own good. It is important that we don't have another tragedy at the location."

Better, surely, that the original tragedy had never occurred, that Castillo's life had been preserved by a more vigilant government that regularly and swiftly condemned properties with such flagrant building code violations. After all, it was not as if this shantytown were new or unique: landlord Jesse Pantoja had owned these shacks for more than forty years, in a sector of town where this form of housing (or worse) had long been the norm. City compliance director Martin Rodríguez would admit not only that similarly dangerous units existed throughout the west and south sides, but also that his office did not have "the manpower to track them all down."

His admission was the most honest thing said during the whole affair. But his words stirred little political response, and the inactivity was not surprising. The city's track record on housing matters—including that of its most lauded public servant, Henry Cisneros—suggested that its leaders have never fully recognized the age-old dimensions of the housing problem. And that means the elderly Castillo would not be the last to die in such untoward conditions.

The scandalously substandard conditions in which many of the city's poor Hispanics lived were a matter of public record in the late nineteenth century. In 1872, poet Sidney Lanier was struck by the premature aging of the city's "Mexican men," who resembled "Old Father Time in reduced circumstances." Those circumstances had deteriorated by 1915, when physicians conducted a public health survey that covered a four-square-mile area just west of downtown—and that not incidentally included Castillo's future neighborhood. There, they stumbled past steaming mounds of "fresh horse manure" which "breed myriads of flies" that not only "swarmed over anything eatable, but into the eyes, noses and mouths of the children as well." When they peered into the appalling jumbles of crude "stalls," they discovered that up to seven people were crammed into six-by-sixteen-foot living spaces; none had running water, adequate sewage, or electricity. "In these miserable abodes with such unsanitary surroundings," the doctors advised the city council, "men, women, and children of all ages are herded together more like swine than human beings."

These shocking revelations made it clear why San Antonio had one of the nation's highest rates of tuberculosis mortality—up to seven times higher than the national average. This chilling data prodded the local board of health to recommend the condemnation of the vast tract of slums, the construction of new housing units, and the enactment of a stringent building "ordinance that will effectually prevent such conditions from arising again." The city council promptly buried the report, as it would a similar one in the late 1920s. The press did its part to deflect attention from the sordid health conditions; the newspapers consistently attributed the high incidence of tuberculosis to consumptives who had migrated to San Antonio to restore their health.

The silence was finally broken in the mid-1930s when another round of exposés of the infamous *corrales*—so called because these hovels often formed a rough U-shape around a communal (and open-air) pit toilet and sink—made it into the national media. These stories also charged that the horrifying housing conditions were responsible for the continued grim mortality rates: no city in the country had more deaths due to tuberculosis, diarrhea, or enteritis. At the epicenter of these deaths, the west side was also repeatedly swept by floods and damaged by fire. The sprawling neighborhood, journalist Ralph Maitland observed in *Century & Forum* magazine, was the "shame of Texas."

The conditions were beyond shameful. Whereas at the beginning of the Great Depression the nation was chastened to learn that one-third of Americans were, in President Franklin Roosevelt's words, ill-fed, ill-clothed, and ill-housed, in San Antonio of the late 1930s that figure amounted to more than half the local population; close to 40,000 families lived in dire straits.

One of those who fought to reverse these depressing statistics was Carmelo Tranchese, a Jesuit priest who in 1932 accepted the pulpit at the Church of Our Lady of Guadalupe, smack in the heart of the west side slums. Having lived in Naples, Italy,

Tranchese thought he had plumbed the depths of the human condition; his new parishioners' despair—their destitution and gnawing hunger—led him deeper still. He began by begging for food and money to feed and clothe his flock, and he spent a good portion of his time lobbying the Roosevelt administration for a share of federal housing dollars to redevelop his dilapidated parish. With the help of Rep. Maury Maverick Sr. and an energized board of health, Tranchese finally convinced Washington of his people's plight. After numerous delays, thirty acres of *corrales* were finally razed to make way for the city's first public housing—and some of the first in the nation: Alazán-Apache Courts. On the city's near-south and east sides other projects were built for its white and black citizens. Upon completion of the Alazán-Apache Courts in 1942, each of its more than 1,000 units had a private bathroom, an amenity that was a luxury in this part of town. Little wonder that Tranchese would be dubbed the "rumpled angel of the slums."

Tranchese's efforts had been miraculous, and if this were a fairy tale their impact would have rippled outward, turning the west side proper into a clean, well-lighted place. Such was not to be. The next cycle of slum clearance did not occur for more than a decade. The slums evocatively known as the "Death Triangle," so named because of their skyrocketing rate of infant mortality, were not rebuilt until the mid-1950s. The intense war effort initially delayed such efforts, and then, in the immediate postwar years, private home developers complained that any increase in the construction of public housing would undercut their market. These rear-guard actions led to an amendment to the city's charter stipulating that "no lands cleared by city slum clearance activities could be sold or used by any public housing agency." Plowing under the *corrales* meant forcing people into the streets.

This no-win situation continued when the pro-business Good Government League (GGL) wrested power from the Democratic machine in the early 1950s. It determined that federal funds would be better utilized refurbishing the downtown core and constructing a series of expressways linking the commercial district to the emerging and northern suburbs. Tearing down substandard housing became a priority only insofar as it facilitated the expansion of the central business district or opened up a low-cost corridor for the new highways. Some, but by no means all, of the former tenants were relocated to new projects in rigorously segregated neighborhoods. These helped reinforce already established land-use patterns that cut along lines of class, ethnicity, race, and age— such as the Villa Tranchese, a 1967 concrete high-rise development for the elderly built hard by the IH-10/IH-35 interchange and named for the angelic "father of public housing." A freeway overlook was not exactly the elevated status Tranchese had hoped new housing initiatives would bring to the community's poor.

Nor could he have expected that such buildings would create a new group of dispossessed—men, women, and children who were evicted from their homes and left to fend for themselves. Their tenuous situation was what so worried Marie McGuire, executive director of the San Antonio Housing Authority (SAHA). When she assumed her duties in 1949, she warned that "any slum clearance program that does not . . . provide decent housing for the unhoused families would be a perversion." Perverted it was. By the late 1950s, for example, SAHA managed roughly 5,100 units, half of which had been built nearly twenty years earlier. This slow rate of construction was reflected in the massive waiting lists each project had accumulated, but SAHA could build no faster than local politics allowed. It was hemmed in by the GGL's developmental politics and forced to locate projects that might only stem the spread of shacks and *corrales* rather than eliminate them and the horrid living conditions they spawned. Under these conditions, the agency barely made a dent in the pressing need for good homes in San Antonio.

The need for affordable housing continued unabated. Despite a spurt of building in the 1970s and 1980s that added another 2,000 units, often through innovative partnerships with private developers, SAHA failed to keep pace with the steady demand for decent accommodations. The waiting lists were as lengthy as ever, suggesting that those clamoring for admittance into the less-than-salubrious, city-controlled apartments or courts lived in even more distressing conditions.

Henry Cisneros, as mayor, was to have swept all this away. Charismatic son of the west side, the first Hispanic to govern the city in the twentieth century, he seemed to represent a new, tough force in San Antonio's hitherto genteel politics. In 1976, while on the city council, which was then wrestling over whether to settle a $150 million lawsuit with Coastal States Gas Corporation, he lashed out at developer Jim Dement, who was urging settlement. Before a packed audience of angry consumers, Cisneros brought the crowd to its feet when he yelled, "Mr. Dement, it's people like you who have had their boot on the neck of my people for generations." His populistic rhetoric and his energetic commitment to revitalize the blighted neighborhoods of the south and west sides were critical in generating a massive turnout of voters in those affected census tracts, a turnout that gave him an ample margin of victory in the 1981 mayoral campaign. With his electoral triumph, as Cisneros biographers Kemper Diehl and Jan Jarboe wrote, "the word went out across the land: The Battle of the Alamo was finally over."

From Cisneros's perspective, that was the wrong language. He much preferred consensus to conflict, and his budgets revealed as much. While he skillfully directed considerable federal funds and local bond monies to street and drainage projects on the long-neglected west and south sides, he also spread the funding around to other, much more affluent sections. This equitable distribution of public spending helped sustain his political prospects, but it also cost him the support of aggressive grassroots organizations such as Communities Organized for Public Services. COPS activists came to believe that the mayor's career ambitions often collided with the needs of San Antonio's most desperate citizens.

Nowhere was this more apparent than in Cisneros's wavering attention to housing for the poor. Although this was one of the issues on which his reputation as an urban reformer had been based, and although he had campaigned regularly on a platform of rebuilding the barrios and ghettos, his rhetorical commitment outstripped his actions.

Rarely proactive, Cisneros tended to respond only to crises. Of this, the September 1984 beating death of a Mr. Johnson on Clark Street is instructive. Notified of the elderly man's death, the mayor raced to the murder scene and, before the television minicams, promised that new homes would replace that east side neighborhood's aged cluster of abandoned buildings and "shooting galleries" so as to protect innocent senior citizens. Although the community's needs were many and great, and some of housing he promised would in time be built—after his mayoralty—he missed the mark on Mr. Johnson. Subsequent investigations indicated that he had been killed in retaliation for a drug deal gone sour. Cisneros's impetuousness in this and other instances, one retired city official observed, could best be characterized as "Fire! Aim! Ready!"

Most of the time, however, housing issues were not even in the mayor's scope. Just how insignificant they had become was evident in Target '90, Cisneros's much-flogged blueprint for San Antonio's future: its few lines about the need for houses were lost in the pages devoted to schemes for how the city should "stake its claim in the giant technological pie." The rapid importation of biomedical professionals and computer manufacturing, not adequate housing, was his nostrum for urban decay.

But then Cisneros was never convinced that large-scale housing redevelopment was an effective prescription for the ills that beset his hometown. Well aware of the magnitude of problems that emanated from such notorious housing projects as Chicago's Cabrini Green, he regularly assailed the evils of high-density warehousing of the poor. About this he was correct, but he managed to miss the larger point: San Antonio was not the Windy City. He frequently (and oddly) blamed the low-level courts for what he believed to be the city's increasing population density.

This reinforced, then, his determination not to replicate the policy failures of other communities, and in so doing he wrote off those most in need of decent, affordable living space.

When instead he touted the prospects of single-family home ownership, believing that this gentrifying panacea would create healthy neighborhoods, he spoke for and to a different class of citizens. Only a select audience were eligible for the houses that have been built through the public-private partnerships he advanced while serving as mayor, later as HUD secretary, and subsequently as a private developer. Two sets of numbers tell the story. As Cisneros indicated in a speech to the National Press Club in April 1996, about 1,000 homes had been built in San Antonio since the early 1970s. But forty to forty-five houses a year is hardly a quick or substantial fix for the city's long-standing housing shortage. The costs associated with these new houses further restricted their impact. Take the Villas de Esperanza, a subdivision that absorbed close to $1 million of HUD funding. The first set of twenty-four homes went on sale in mid-February 1997 at a cost ranging from the high forties to the high fifties (that's thousands), prices that placed these "low cost" houses at or above the city's median housing prices. The Villas, and the clean space they represented, were thus a financial stretch for the working poor. Though financial institutions were compelled to offer low-cost loans to help potential buyers with their down payments, qualifying for those loans was nearly impossible for the urban underclass.

This population never figured large in Cisneros's political calculus, and they did not disturb his imagination after he moved to Los Angeles to head up Univision. Those who lured him to this new job did so hoping he would help attract a larger middle-class Hispanic audience to the Spanish network. Cisneros eagerly embraced this rich opportunity to raise this target group's profile and, through more refined television programming, show them how to "make it in the United States." There was unintended irony in this uplifting claim: it was uttered on the day that city bulldozers flattened Serefino Castillo's burned-out home.

POLITICAL TEMPER

Republican Sheik

There is an old joke about two European Jews sitting on a park bench during the 1930s. One demanded to know why the other pored over the anti-Semitic ravings of the fascist press. "Well," his friend replied, "when I read the Jewish newspapers, I get depressed. All I hear about are our troubles, about how persecuted we are. But the fascists write that we are a great and powerful people. Why, we control the international banking system, drive powerful rulers to their knees, and conspire to dominate the world! Which news would you rather read?"

This wonderfully subversive commentary on the tangled relationship between victims and victimizers came to mind when I listened to some startling television commentary in June 1993 following the death of a local hero and native son, John Connally. The former governor of Texas would have been president of the United States, a reporter asserted, had it not been for the Jews.

The scandalous claim that Jews robbed Connally of his rightful place in the American political firmament emerged in an

interview with family members that was given considerable play
on the local nightly news just hours after Big John's demise.
Speaking from a lawn chair overlooking the family ranch in
Floresville, county seat of Wilson County, immediately south of
San Antonio, one of Connally's brothers argued that Jewish voters
had broken with Connally in 1979 when he offered a controversial
Middle East peace proposal. They "dropped him cold," this griev-
ing sibling averred, in response to Connally's assertion that there
were "two sides" to the Arab-Israeli conflict. The Jews' subsequent
opposition destroyed Connally's campaign, teaching the South
Texas Republican something European fascists knew a generation
ago: this stiff-necked people are a relentless, powerful force.

Political life is never so simple. Connally had failed to capture
the White House for any number of reasons, including a troubled
past and a volatile personality. His famed speech on the Middle
East, then, was but one element in a larger set of problems. The
problems began with the man, or at least the voters' perceptions of
him, according to James Reston's riveting biography of Connally,
The Lone Star (1988). From the moment he announced his candidacy, he was attacked as yet another Lone Star "wheeler-dealer," a
larger-than-life caricature who spent freely, hobnobbed with the
corporate jet set, and pandered to the little people. His public
image had been soured further by memories of bribery charges
leveled against him in the early 1970s; it was alleged that he had
accepted $10,000 from the milk-products industry—and al-
though he was acquitted, the stain remained. Texas satirist Cactus
Pryor, for one, feigned astonishment that Connally would have

accepted a bribe so small: "Why he spends that much every week on hair spray."

A too-slick Connally was a tough sell in post-Watergate America, a society that yearned for honesty in public life as much as it did for fiscal restraint, a diminished bureaucracy, and lower taxes. Moreover, Connally had to overcome doubts about his political opportunism: this born-again Republican had never been fully accepted by die-hard members of his new political base. He received a rude lesson in the costs of becoming a chameleon while campaigning in New Hampshire in March 1979. The Granite State's right-wing press savaged him, particularly William Loeb, the cranky and crusty publisher of the *Manchester Union*, who called Connally a "veteran Democrat of the LBJ era in Texas" who puts on "a wonderful looking front, but it is all on the surface."

Connally was also accused of being unpatriotic. "In the last few years Connally has done most of his wheeling and dealing with oil-wealthy Arabs of the Middle East," Loeb editorialized. "He might be called the Arab's candidate for the President of the United States." This incendiary attack is important for several reasons: it came from a state, like many northern ones, that had been badly burned during the 1973 Arab oil boycott and that therefore resented the Sunbelt oil wealth Connally seemed to represent. And Loeb's criticisms came seven months before Connally delivered his pivotal Middle East address. The potential consequences of the candidate's foreign policy were already under fire.

At issue had been Connally's 1977 purchase of the Main Street Bank of Houston with two Arab sheiks, a business relationship that netted him considerable wealth. It also got him into trouble: "Connally [now] had a direct, personal and financial stake in a cozy relationship with the Arab world," biographer Reston observed, and that in turn meant that he had taken on a "serious, if not catastrophic, political liability." Few in the American electorate would mistake him for a "disinterested statesman."

His partisanship emerged in the late summer of 1979 when public opinion polls showed him falling well behind Ronald Reagan. Hoping to distinguish himself from the aged front-runner, and calculating that a pro-Arab posture on the Middle East peace process might divide Jewish and black voters and draw the latter to his standard, Connally decided to give the most important speech of his political life. It contained three planks: Israel was to withdraw to its 1967 borders, the "moderate" Arab states would recognize Israel's right to exist, and Jerusalem would become an "international" city. There was little new in the speech—the previous four presidents had said similar things— but it generated a firestorm.

Hot on Connally's case were the usual demons in the conservative cosmology—the *New York Times* and the *New Republic*— as well as an odd set of devils. Christian fundamentalists rapidly deserted him, including the wife of his campaign manager, believing that he had become, in Reston's words, "the candidate of the infidels." The Jewish response was no less swift, but not because of his infidelity; Connally had in fact counted on their anger. As speechwriter Sam Hoskinson remembered, "Connally knew it was a risk, but he knew we weren't getting any contributions from the Jewish community." The Jews had not turned on Connally; he had turned on them.

That John Connally's brother thought otherwise is not surprising. What made his argument of a Jewish conspiracy so comforting and compelling was that it had absolved his late brother of responsibility for his many political failings. Fantasy is a blessed antidote to reality, which is exactly what that mythical Jew on the park bench recognized.

Hill Country Nazis

"I never in my life, except perhaps, in awakening from a dream, met with such a sudden and complete transfer of associations," Frederick Law Olmsted said when he and his brother rode into "Neu Braunfels," Texas, in early 1854. As he gazed upon the tiny community, located thirty miles north of San Antonio, and took in its built landscape of "small, low cottages, of no pretensions to elegance," watched its industrious inhabitants at work, and encountered their polite and refined ways, he felt transported back in time and space. "We were in Germany," he concluded, almost in disbelief, much like the Rhineland he and his brother had tramped some years before, and which they would "ever remember gratefully."

An abolitionist who had traveled throughout the South, Olmsted was especially fascinated that this humble German settlement raised cotton, and did so more efficiently than the slave-based producers of the crop he had studied in eastern Texas and the Old South. This "FREE-LABOR COTTON," he enthused, "had been judiciously cultivated, and had yielded a fine crop, differing, however, from what we had noticed on the plantations the day before, in this circumstance—the picking had been entirely completed, and with care and exactness, so that none of the cotton . . . had been left to waste." With their free-soil convictions, sense of civic responsibility, and liberal political commitments, the German Texans were for Olmsted the perfect antidotes to an oppressive southern slavocracy.

So taken was he with the progressive character of the small enclave that for years afterward he continued to scheme with Adolph Douai, editor of the *San Antonio Zeitung*, to launch a utopian colony in the hills west of New Braunfels. Given his faith in the beauty of the land and the strength of its people's character, Olmsted would surely have been sorely disappointed to learn that some late-twentieth-century Germans living in New Braunfels bore none of their ancestors' virtues. But not half as disappointed as Debbie Biggers.

A teacher at New Braunfels High School, Biggers wanted to put a human face on the traumas of World War Two, a conflagration her adolescent charges could not have known firsthand. But when she invited San Antonian Eric Haas, a Holocaust survivor, to talk to her classes and share his memories of the brutal years he spent in a German concentration camp, she and her students received a baptism by fire: the war, they learned, had not ended.

At least not for those citizens of the town who deny the Holocaust happened. The deniers bombarded the *New Braunfels Herald-Zeitung* with telephone calls and correspondence challenging the newspaper's decision to publish an account of Biggers's special class and Haas's participation in it. Some denounced what they called the insulting, anti-German sentiment of the article, another doubted whether Haas was old enough to have been alive in the 1940s, and a third smeared him as a "habitual liar." Biggers, who had worried that her teenagers needed a dose of reality before embarking on their study of the war, had unintentionally uncovered the degree to which some adults willfully wished away the troubling past.

The most willful was a woman of German descent who, whether she knew it or not, linked contemporary anti-Semitism and Holocaust denial to the 1930s fascism that gave birth to the horrors of Nazi Germany. She did so by describing Jews as "vampires, living off Christians," behavior that explained, she said, a curious fact: after the war Jews had flooded into the United States, not Israel. "Vampires can't live off of other vampires," she said.

This shocking image has had a dark past. In the 1930s, American fascists used the same imagery to stir animosity over the possible influx into the United States of European Jews fleeing Nazi persecution. I had stumbled upon this connection several months earlier when my sister-in-law's mother called to ask if I could confirm whether Benjamin Franklin was a flaming anti-Semite. Stunned by her question, I remained stunned as she described a speech Franklin allegedly had delivered to the Constitutional Convention in 1787. In "The Jewish Race: A Prophecy," which gave vent to some of the most vicious anti-Semitism I have ever heard, Franklin reportedly warned against the "grave danger"

America faced if it did not close its borders to Jewish immigrants. Unwilling to return to Palestine—"they are vampires and vampires cannot live on other vampires . . . they must live on Christians and other people who do not belong to their race"—the Jews wanted to flock instead to the New World and "destroy us by changing our form of government, for which we Americans shed our blood and sacrificed our lives, our properties and personal freedom." Once here, they would reduce future generations to a kind of fiscal slavery: "Within two hundred years our children will be working in the fields to feed them, while they remain in the counting houses gleefully rubbing their hands." Failure to exclude "the Jews forever," Franklin apparently warned his fellow conventioneers, would lead "your children and your children's children [to] curse you in your graves."

Were any of this obscene rhetoric true, I realized as I hung up the phone, then the Franklin I thought I knew and admired (our first child was named partly in his honor) was a fraud. Happily, no revision was necessary. The next morning, after an intense search through my university's library, I located a reference to the speech's fraudulence that led me to its genesis in the mid-1930s. According to the eminent historian Charles Beard, who broke the story in the *Jewish Frontier* (March 1935), the "Prophecy" first appeared in a fascist publication, *The Liberator*, published in Asheville, North Carolina. It was swiftly picked up and republished in the European anti-Semitic press, coverage that heightened its newsworthiness so that it reappeared in a host of American right-wing venues. The so-called "Prophecy" was tainted with illegitimacy.

Its language was stained by fraudulence, too. As Beard recognized, its linguistic patterns were not Franklin's. Nothing in its tone, diction, and vocabulary or its overt hostility matched any other of the great stylist's addresses. There were other internal discrepancies: the document came with what purported to be authentic references that in fact revealed its literary duplicity. An introductory comment, for example, indicated that a copy of the speech was located in the journal of Charles Pinckney of South Carolina, and a concluding note cited its presence in the Franklin Institute in Philadelphia. After checking both repositories and finding no similar document, and then analyzing Franklin's published writings and private letters, Beard concluded that the founding father had never expressed "such sentiments against the Jews as are ascribed to him by the Nazis—American and German." What my sister-in-law's mother had uncovered was, in Beard's words, a "barefaced forgery."

How then did this old lie gain new life? It owes its resurrection to modern technology. The "Franklin Prophecy" is now readily available, for the version I saw was downloaded from an Internet location in Israel. Given the world's access to the Internet, anyone anywhere can read this patently false piece of anti-Semitic propaganda. Moreover, it will attract a new generation of avid readers in search of justification for their hate from among the neo-Nazi movements in Europe and North America, and from their noisy fellow travelers, the Holocaust deniers. It is particularly appalling that one of America's most benign and funny men should be made to support their jackbooted viciousness.

That prospect disturbed many in the 1930s too, but at least they felt they could counteract the impact of this falsehood. When the editor of the *Pennsylvania Magazine of History and Biography* in 1937 excerpted Charles Beard's commentary further to expose the fraud, he wrote that the mere act of exposure ought to be "sufficient to prevent any further misunderstanding of Franklin's attitudes toward the Jews."

In our brave and vast new world of high-speed Internet connectivity, we can have no such faith. Just ask Debbie Biggers.

Lone Star

Oh, how I miss Henry B. Henry B. Gonzalez, that is—the long-time congressman from San Antonio who died in late 2000. For all his faults—and he had his share—Gonzalez was rarely at a loss for words, especially when confronted with actions he believed were unjust and unwise. These concerns led him to take the floor of the Texas Senate in May 1957 and mount a now-famous filibuster. He and Sen. Abraham "Chick" Kazan talked for thirty-six hours to thwart a bill that would maintain school segregation in Texas in defiance of the Supreme Court's *Brown v. Board of Education* decision of 1954. "Are we not the duly elected representatives of all citizens," he shouted, "including the Negro who is a citizen, pays his taxes and bears arms like all of us?" Drawing on the venerable history of his home city—"I am from San Antonio, the cradle of Texas Liberty"—Gonzalez asked whether his fellow representatives were concerned only with "the liberty of Anglo Americans." He assumed so and pitched his voice "to register the plaintive cry, the dumb protest of the inarticulate minorities who feel they lack representation."

So Henry B. would continue to feel and act during his thirty-seven-year tenure in the U.S. House of Representatives. A staunch supporter of federal funding for education and housing, a bedrock concern for his poor constituents on San Antonio's west side, he fought just as tirelessly for state and federal investment in the downtown tourist economy, notably for HemisFair '68, which had brought much-needed attention to the Riverwalk. He advocated as well for Model City dollars for community redevelopment initiatives. As his congressional seniority grew, his committee assignments expanded in scope and significance. Tapped to be chair of the House Banking, Finance, and Urban Affairs Committee in the late 1980s, he helped clean up the Savings and Loan debacle and passed legislation that established the National Housing Trust.

Along the way, he riled his opponents, needled the often cozy relationship that developed between the Democratic and Republican congressional leadership, and was a special pain to the White House. When President Reagan sent troops into Grenada in 1983, Henry B. called for his impeachment. He demanded it again when investigations into the Iran-Contra scandals of the late 1980s implicated the president and his staff in subverting Congress's constitutional role in setting the contours of U.S. foreign policy. As Reagan's successors would discover, Gonzalez was just as ready to challenge their putative prerogatives to make war.

The call came late at night, pulling Bertha Gonzalez, Henry B.'s wife, from a deep sleep. "What time is your husband coming home?" the voice demanded. "I'm going to wait for him and put a bullet between his eyes." That was only one of many threats, all triggered when, on January 16, 1991, just hours before the first Persian Gulf War officially began, Gonzalez introduced a resolution to impeach President George H. W. Bush.

Its five articles pulled no punches. Gonzalez charged, among other things, that the president had violated the equal protection clause of the Constitution, had broken international law when he bribed and intimidated member states of the United Nations to gain support for "belligerent acts" against Iraq, and would commit war crimes through a massive aerial bombardment that would murder innocent civilians. On top of that, Bush had shredded the U.S. Constitution, Gonzalez declared, when he "systematically eliminated every option for a peaceful resolution" of the crisis, "rendering any substantive debate by Congress meaningless." These "high crimes and misdemeanors" could only be dealt with through impeachment, the Texas congressman believed, and he called upon his colleagues to stand up to Bush "on behalf of the soldiers who will die, the civilians who will be massacred, and the Constitution that will be destroyed."

The wonder is not that these words provoked death threats but that they garnered so little national media coverage. Neither the *New York Times* nor the *Washington Post* acknowledged that Gonzalez had submitted the articles of impeachment. More amazing still was the fact that the *Post*, two days after their submission, blandly observed that among congressional members "outright opposition to the war was rare." So rare that the only congressional figures it claimed continued to tout peace were (anti) warhorses Ron Dellums (D-CA) and Bernard Sanders (I-VT).

Gonzalez was not invisible in the San Antonio press. The two major newspapers of the day, the Hearst-owned *San Antonio Light* and the Murdoch-owned *San Antonio Express-News*, carried stories about his legislative initiative, but, true to form, they were especially captivated by the sensational, night-time threat on his life; the legal challenge his call for impeachment represented went unacknowledged. When the threats ended, so did the story, and within two days the issue disappeared from the news pages. It blossomed anew in letters to the editor, where Gonzalez's patriotism was impugned and his manhood derided. These attacks were consistent with the city's demographics: known as the "mother of the army," San Antonio was ringed by five major military bases and countless minor installations and peopled with a significant number of military retirees. In this town, where church billboards commanded passersby to "Pray for Victory" and yellow ribbons everywhere symbolized support for American troops in the Middle East, Gonzalez was no hero.

Others knew well the dilemmas of being antiwar in one of the nation's most martial metropoli. "It's tough being an activist in San Antonio," conceded Graciela Sanchez, director of the Esperanza Peace and Justice Center, which sponsored weekly demonstrations at the federal courthouse and coordinated rallies communitywide. The extensive military presence, she noted, coupled with the "very conservative" influence of the Catholic Church, limited the numbers and thus the visibility of the protestors.

It was all the more remarkable, therefore, that Gonzalez's articles of impeachment did not become a rallying cry in 1991 for San Antonians committed to peace in the Persian Gulf. But they did not. Neither Gonzalez's name nor his activities surfaced, for example, at teach-ins at local colleges and universities. When I asked some students at a rally what they thought of Henry B.'s resolution, they replied, "Who's he?"

Who indeed. But then Gonzalez was used to being ignored. When he filed articles of impeachment against Ronald Reagan for the Iran-Contra scandal, they too had been dismissed, leading many to conclude that he was nothing but a crank.

Certainly some of his behavior over the preceding years had been quirky. His speeches tended to wander (like his mind, said his critics), and his quick temper contributed to the sense that his best days were behind him. In 1986 he threw a punch at a restaurant patron who, when Gonzalez walked by, had called him "our No. 1 leading damn communist." As a sign of its disaffection with his candidacy, the *Express-News* stopped endorsing him for re-election, something it once had done regularly.

Was Gonzalez's call for Bush's impeachment yet another sign of his having lost touch with reality? Quite the contrary: it was based on his deep convictions about the proper relationship between the government and its people, and his unshakable commitment to the nation's democratic ethos. As Maury Maverick Jr., a longtime friend and civil rights advocate, put it at the time, "Henry B. hates thieves, whether they're liberal or conservative." Demanding the impeachment of American presidents was part of that.

Gonzalez had other reasons for being adamant about Bush's impeachment, however. In 1964, he had voted for the Gulf of Tonkin resolution, which granted President Lyndon Johnson unlimited power to wage war in Vietnam. The San Antonio congressman apparently deeply regretted that decision, Maverick reported in 1991: "His conscience [was] bothering him." In making certain he did not repeat his earlier mistake, Gonzalez hoped to prick the national conscience, hardly the act of a man past his prime.

He seemed just as sharp in June 1993 when President Bill Clinton launched twenty-three Tomahawk cruise missiles at the headquarters of the Iraqi intelligence agency—devastating payback for Sadaam Hussein's attempt to assassinate President Bush. When news of the predawn assault filtered back to San Antonio, the city held its breath. Not because of any innate sympathy for Saddam Hussein's dread secret service, and not as a result of empathy for the innocent Iraqi civilians who, once again, were caught in the crossfire between our warring nations. Nor, in this conservative American city, was our pause in inhalation a response to concerns over the attack's political ramifications for that infamous noninhaler, Bill Clinton. No, we were waiting to hear what Henry B. would have to say.

Our pause made sense: Gonzalez had often fulminated against the mindless actions, political grasping, and ethically bankrupt behavior so characteristic of Beltway life. And he had thrived during the twelve years of the Reagan-Bush Republican rule, which had given him ample time to sharpen his ability to puncture pretense, sniff out hypocrisy, and, occasionally, go off the deep end.

But the question left hanging was this: once the Democrats controlled the White House, would Gonzalez play the good soldier and bite back his criticism of this president's overseas adventurism?

Not a chance. In an interview with the local press, Gonzalez took sharp exception to the Clinton administration's violent retaliation for Iraq's plot to assassinate President Bush. This wasn't just "an act of war," Henry B. fumed, "it is an act of insanity." What struck him as so crazed was the veil of virtue that the president so easily threw over the Tomahawk attack, a veil that for Gonzalez masked the similarities between the American reprisal and Iraq's brutal, if botched, plans. "The idea that the United States, through acts of terrorism, is killing innocent women and children is wrong, morally wrong," he said.

This conclusion did not mean that Clinton would soon find a Gonzalez-inspired impeachment resolution circulating on the House floor. "Being gormless is not an impeachable offense," the legislator asserted. Puzzled by his recondite vocabulary? Before you reach for your *Webster's,* here's a hint: those who launch "smart" bombs aren't.

After years of calling chief executives on the carpet, and decades of challenging those in power to do better and more for those in need, this man of modest means and dogged determination must have been galled by President Clinton's sexual peccadilloes. But Gonzalez did not mistake human failings—however troubling—for high crimes and misdemeanors. And on his last day as a member of the U.S. House of Representatives, he voted against the impeachment of William Jefferson Clinton.

FUTURE TENSE

Breathe Uneasy

Here's a shock: I love driving in Houston. What sounds like a contradiction in terms is not. The nation's fourth largest city offers up a unique visual drama that compensates for its frequently car-clogged freeways. It makes up, too, for the long haul from San Antonio. After three hours of pushing the pedal to the metal on Interstate 10 (which makes our Toyota Corolla sound faster than it is), my mind is a blank; as for my eyes, well, they're wasted from staring out over the monotonous, flat coastal plain. By the time I hit the western suburb of Katy, I'm more than ready for a little uplift.

Downtown Houston complies. Its soaring glass-sheathed towers and stone-clad monoliths, with their varied geometric shape, tint, and volume, fill the windshield with a rich profusion of light, color, and form. That is by design, of course, for these buildings are best seen at high speeds, and it is a joy to spin off IH-10, head south on IH-45, and then swing north along U.S. 59, a route that allows drivers to wrap around the central business district and catch the play of angle, shadow, and glow.

But the energetic spectacle that welcomes weary travelers to the Bayou City only works if we can see the dazzling skyline. That is more difficult, I realized the last time I wheeled down the elevated freeways, as a consequence of Houston's deteriorating air quality. The root causes have been clear since the 1970s, when the city was first slapped for violating the Clean Air Act. The degree of its nonattainment status has only intensified over the past three decades, due to the high level of auto and truck emissions and industrial pollutants. With more than 3.74 million registered cars logging an estimated 70 million vehicle miles daily, it is no wonder that emissions swirl together into a toxic soup that, when trapped in a nasty air inversion, produces a poisonous dark cloud.

It's bad enough that this thick smog obscures the city's architectural wonderland, but who wants to vie with Los Angeles for the nation's worst pollution? Who wants a population of compromised lungs and diminished lives?

The Texas Natural Resources Conservation Commission (TNRCC), for one. TNRCC, whose legion of critics calls it Train Wreck (perhaps one reason its name was changed in 2003 to the Texas Commission on Environmental Quality), monitors and regulates air-quality standards statewide. But it has regularly gambled with the public's health. In 1998, the Environmental Protection Agency toxic release categories revealed that Texans breathed some of the most polluted air in the country. That had long been true, according to *Grandfathered Pollution: The Dirty Secret of Texas Industries* (1998), a report issued by a statewide environmental coalition, because of the emissions exemptions granted to industry in the 1971 Texas Clean Air Act. This bill allowed companies to release vast quantities of toxins into the atmosphere; its regulatory legislation left the petrochemical industry unregulated, devastating air quality and lung capacity.

So it should not come as much of a surprise that TNRCC also waffled on the amount and impact of auto emissions. Take, for instance, its June 2002 decision to rescind the speed limit of fifty-five miles per hour on Houston highways, which it earlier had imposed to meet EPA-mandated clean air levels. Its June 5 press release announcing the change, cleverly entitled "Houston Clean Air Strategy Enhanced," sought to reassure locals that "intense scientific scrutiny" had revealed that mandated reductions in car speed had a negligible effect on lowering the levels of highly dangerous nitrogen oxides. According to TNRCC and Houston boosters, an EPA-sponsored study released in January 2002 indicated that a reduction in auto and truck speed had a negligible impact on nitrogen oxide emissions. But TNRCC did not acknowledge that this new finding, based on an upgraded EPA emissions modeling system called Mobile 6, was itself preliminary; it needed to be more widely field tested before the EPA could validate its legitimacy. Neither did it admit that this technique had not been tested in Houston, nor that Mobile 6's generalized projections revealed that there is in fact a correlation between speed and nitrogen oxide emissions, just a smaller one than previously supposed. So much for "scientific scrutiny."

Worse was that TNRCC failed to note that nitrogen oxides, a generic term for a set of highly reactive gasses dangerous to public health, are only one element of the EPA's list of six principal tailpipe pollutants. Would lifting the speed limit to seventy miles per hour have a "negligible" impact on the amount of lead, carbon monoxide, sulfur dioxide, particulate matter, and volatile organic compounds? Hardly. "Almost every car and truck burns less fuel per mile traveling at 55 mph than at 70 mph," observed Alan Clark, transportation planner for the Houston-Galveston Area Council. "Because you're burning less fuel, you're emitting less air pollution."

Perhaps that maxim was too difficult for TNRCC to grasp, but it was not science (new or otherwise) that led to its hasty retreat in Houston. It was politics. The moment its original, December 2001 decision to lower speed limits was announced, it ran into a series of roadblocks. Brazoria and Fort Bend Counties sued in state district court to halt enforcement in those political jurisdictions. The Business Coalition for Clean Air Appeals Group—a petrochemical lobby—filed suit in the same district court, challenging TNRCC's decision to force them to cut back on industrial emissions. Even Harris County District Attorney Chuck Rosenthal let slip in the spring of 2002 that taking motorists ticketed for speeding to a jury trial would work to the *defendant's* advantage, a thinly veiled effort to sabotage the law's enforcement. And then there was the antienvironmental congressional cabal: Tom Delay (R-Houston) and his fellow local Republican representatives fired off a stiff public rebuke of TNRCC's actions.

The commission broke before the assault. "There is no question there has been a large amount of requests [to repeal the limit] from elected officials," TNRCC Chair Robert Huston admitted to the *Houston Chronicle.* "There has been a huge public outcry. Of course we responded to that." The commission always has.

Two years earlier, when the commission had an opportunity to adopt California's tougher emissions standards (which, not incidentally, would reduce nitrogen oxide emission levels by 25 percent), it refused to do so after auto industry lobbyists and their Republican minions applied considerable pressure to block the regulations. The commission's historically weak position on air pollution—industrial and automotive—reinforced criticism that it was little committed to the broader public good.

In a state as heavily urbanized as Texas (more than 80 percent of its populace lives in cities—the largest percentage in the union), wreaking havoc with air-quality standards in Houston has statewide implications. San Antonio, for example, has been flirting for years with EPA nonattainment air-quality status. Each time TNRCC has folded before the politically powerful, its capitulation has signaled to the South Texas metropolis that there is little regulatory incentive to clean up its increasingly brown-smeared skies. And that lack of coercive pressure feeds into San Antonio's traditional response to pressing environmental issues and developmental problems—to not respond until compelled to do so. Its unwillingness to proactively grapple with air pollution is of a piece with its historic resistance to resolving threats to the Edwards Aquifer recharge zone, its multiyear stall on enacting a tough tree preservation ordinance, and its inability to deal with sprawl.

These concerns are bound up with the fact that San Antonio,

like Houston, Dallas, Forth Worth, and Austin, is addicted to the
car. In 1990, there were nearly 875,000 automobiles registered in
Bexar County, or 1.36 people per car; as of November 2001, there
were 1.49 million cars, or .99 people per car. More cars, plus more
drivers, equals greater air pollution and a level of emissions that,
as Houston and Los Angeles have amply demonstrated, has devastating effects on communal health and life span.

There remains this hope: that San Antonio's accelerating
automobility runs afoul of the EPA's strengthened regulatory
authority. In 2002, the U.S. Supreme Court and the U.S. Court of
Appeals gave the federal agency the green light to issue and en-
force even more stringent air-quality standards. If enacted, these
new regulations would have a real-life impact. According to the
American Lung Association, tougher controls of auto emissions
would, among other outcomes, prevent upward of 15,000 premature deaths and perhaps as many as 350,000 cases of aggravated
asthma. Johns Hopkins University researcher Jonathan Samet
goes further, indicating that the recent data implicates air pollution as a trigger and a cause for asthma outbreaks, which have
grown at a startling rate since 1980. In 2003, *OnEarth* reports,
more than three times as many Americans suffer from restricted
lung capacity than was documented when Ronald Reagan entered
the White House. To reverse this unhealthy situation, Samet and
his colleagues aver, will require stronger regulatory control of
tailpipe emissions.

That is good news, oddly, for it might prove a potent rebuttal
to those entrenched national, state, and local politicians, and to
TNRCC bureaucrats, for whom clean air seems such a dirty idea.

Tourism, Inc.

Amid a heated reelection campaign in March 1997, Mayor Bill Thornton did something curious: he told a truth. In defending his support of tax abatements for a proposed downtown Sheraton Hotel, he argued that the low-skill jobs the new building would generate were an exact match for the city's undereducated workforce. "Unfortunately, there is a great number of adults in our community that are defined as functionally illiterate," he said in a news conference. He concluded that using tax abatements to lure only high-paying jobs to town, as his campaign rivals proposed, was unrealistic. It was "naive to expect much of San Antonio's workforce to step into management or technical positions."

With these words, the mayor touched off a firestorm that consumed his political career. Although none of Thornton's opponents directly challenged his argument's accuracy, they pounced on its political implications. His four challengers pledged to support a moratorium on tax abatements, and a revision of the city code, so that future abatements would be tied to the production of a "living wage." Grassroots organizations turned up the heat, and so furious was the response that within a week Thornton appeared to backpedal, proposing an ordinance that would ban tax abatements. "We are not going to do phase-ins for any more hotels," he confirmed. His waffling undercut his credibility and was partly responsible for his failure to make that spring's electoral runoff. He came in third in the primary to the eventual victor, councilman Howard Peak.

What neither the soon-to-be-ousted mayor nor his many critics explained was why San Antonio was such a low-wage, cheap-labor town. The answer lies in the powerful role tourism plays in the modern economy. The city's dedication to servicing an ever-larger number of visitors has compelled it to build up a complex infrastructure that includes historic landmarks such as the Alamo and four other Spanish Era missions, the Riverwalk and convention center, and theme parks, hotels, restaurants, and bars. The investment has paid off in this respect: tourism is said to contribute upward of $4 billion to the community's coffers. Yet the bargain the city has struck with itself through its focus on tourism comes at a decisive cost: the creation of an increasing number of low-skilled positions that provide necessary entry-level work for those with minimal education, but that have done, and will do, little to enhance their economic prospects. Thornton and his opponents were caught in a vicious cycle of their own making.

There was nothing new in the anxious warnings some citizens voiced about tourism's profound social consequences. The sources of their worries can be traced back to the economic choices San Antonians have made since the mid-nineteenth century. For better and for worse, and at considerable expense, San Antonio has long catered to its visitors.

Cattle were our first tourists. Following the Civil War, when the great annual drives moved up from the South Texas grasslands and swung past town on their way north to Kansas railheads, every new set of thundering hooves reinforced a pattern of behavior that has persisted, regardless of species. The swelling herds rumbled through town at peak season—the winter and spring; they guzzled vast quantities of food and drink; and occasionally they got out of hand, endangering life, limb, and property. Residents, fearing for their safety, complained about the bovines' bellowing presence and worried about their deleterious impact on community values. Yet they also banked on their continued movement along the many trails that converged on San Antonio, for the economic payoff of this quadrapedal tourism was considerable.

The cattle were a loss leader. The real money was captured in the spending habits of their human tenders. The drovers and *vaqueros* spent freely in the many hotels, saloons, and gambling emporia built to meet their needs. In 1892, with a resident population of about 30,000, San Antonio had nearly 300 bars, a ratio that bespoke the city's central preoccupation with hawking its wares to those just passing through.

Selling sexual favors to this transient population was just as lucrative. Releasing sexual energy whetted the cowboys' appetite for material consumption (and vice versa); they came and shopped, but especially shopped, busily purchasing accessories essential to their trade—rifles, revolvers, and bullets; chaps, hats, boots, and spurs; saddles and harnesses. As this commercial traffic developed, it had an important spatial consequence, focusing trade on the western edge in an area that would later be called Cattlemen's Square.

By that name, San Antonio acknowledged its intimate relationship with ranching. Newspapers reinforced this connection by rustling up anecdotes about cowboy conduct that had long been part of the community's lore. Publishing these tales—the hard-won ranching fortunes that vanished with the casual roll of the dice, the flush cowpuncher who soaked in a bath of champagne— added luster to the marketing of the late-nineteenth-century city. Visitors added their two bits. Harriet Spofford, for one, swooned over the grizzled rider who "on his way northward with his bunch of cattle, has stopped in 'Santone' for a frolic." Although "unkempt and unshorn, filthy and ragged and very drunk," no Texan mistakes "these vaqueros, in their big boots and old blouses and rough beards, as mere vagabonds at loose ends," she assured the genteel readers of *Harper's Monthly*. "He knows that it is ten to one that the shabbiest on the plaza will draw his check for $100,000 to-day to pay for the cattle he has just bought to improve his stock." By passing on this bit of gilded frontier lore, Spofford exported the notion of San Antonio as a rough-and-tumble Old West town.

This late-nineteenth-century publicity was also a literary sign of the frontier's passing. An economic signal lay in the collapse of the cattle rush itself. By the early 1880s, due to intense overgrazing, difficulties in transporting cattle to distant urban markets, and the desire for cheaper and greener grass, many of the region's herds, and the capital derived from their production, moved to the northern plains. San Antonio was left in the lurch. Much of the business infrastructure, built in the boom years to separate trail riders from their disposable income, withered. Dependency on this drive-by tourism left the city vulnerable to market vagaries.

Making it even more vulnerable was its support of the chimera that impelled other humans to the city, people dying to take advantage of what they were told was the climate's restorative powers. Die they would: those suffering from tuberculosis who first trailed into this frontier health resort in the late 1840s were no more cured by the salubrious environment than the thousands who later followed. Yet in their care, and demise, there was money to be made, and the community was not slow in realizing a grisly profit from this trade. When investors in the late 1880s funneled considerable capital into the construction of health care facilities, however, they unwittingly gave succor to a set of dire public health consequences that would threaten the commonweal.

This new form of tourism depended on bad science. The nineteenth-century medical prescription for tuberculosis hinged on a simple environmental determinism: pure air, clean water, and warm climes brought relief to the suffering and might cure the afflicted. Actually, nothing about this regime enhanced the prospects of the victims of the "white plague," but its vagueness played into the hands of boosters. They touted the Southwest's medicinal weather, hoping to entice those whose lungs and throats were unhappily compromised. One 1850s convalescent, who had dragged himself to San Antonio after years of protracted illness, claimed that within two months he had been revived from the dead because of the weather: "This improvement I attribute to the purer, dry, light atmosphere which prevails here the greater part of the time." Others praised the virtues of the "ozone," a gas said to be so plentiful that it was as much a curative for human lungs as it was for meat. How else explain, an 1880s health resort pamphlet declared, "the bodies of hundreds of thousands of dead animals lying on the prairie [which] emit no odor whatever."

Promotional agents were not the only ones untroubled by the facts: an uncritical, hacking horde hustled south and west in response to these airy assertions, among them poet Sidney Lanier. Traveling "as valet to his right lung—a service in which he has been engaged some years," he arrived in December 1872. Although he would cast doubt on the stability of the region's weather, and thus on "its alleged happy influence on consumption," he was not immune to the charms of this "growing resort for consumptives." With others "sent here from remote parts of the United States and from Europe, and who may be seen on fine days, in various stages of decrepitude, strolling along the streets," Lanier indulged in the curative potions heavily advertised in local newspapers. "I have been taking Möller's Cod Liver Oil regularly three times a day for a month," he advised his wife, and then as a chaser he drained "from three to six doses of pure whiskey (the best, by the way, I have ever seen)."

Such nostrums only depressed another tubercular-ridden writer—William Sydney Porter (O. Henry)—who lashed out at the city in his short story "A Fog in Santone." The tale opens with a consumptive, his "white face half-concealed by the high-turned overcoat collar," trying to wheedle morphine tablets from a suspicious drugstore clerk. Rebuffed, he decides the thirty-six pills he already has are sufficient to end his life now, a suicidal impulse brought on by the "gray mist" that earlier had swept up the river, "an opaque terror" clutching at his throat. His death is temporarily put on hold, however, through the kind ministrations of Miss Rosa, a prostitute working one of the saloons he stumbles into. With the requisite heart of gold, she cheers this cheerless man and sends him home with new hope for a sunnier day, after relieving him of his cache of drugs. The dark, final act in her young life has just begun. In a classic O. Henry twist, the bar girl crushes the morphine into her drink and stirs up the fatal concoction with her hat pin.

This grim end deftly pricks the conceit that underlay San Antonio's tubercular hustle. "It had been computed that three thousand invalids were hibernating in the town," O. Henry wrote, lured here to bathe in the "goddess Ozone." That it brought no relief did not trouble the local citizenry: "Santone . . . cannot be blamed for this cold gray fog that came and kissed the lips of the three thousand, and then delivered them to the cross," O. Henry declared. No, it was not culpable for the fact that here many of "the wooers of ozone capitulated"; it was not the city's fault that on "the red streams of Hemorrhagia a few souls drifted away, leaving behind pathetic heaps, white and chill as the fog itself." O. Henry's sardonic take unmasked the city's grotesque willingness to sell tuberculosis victims down the river, all for the sake of a buck.

The town criers hastened to repair the damage through guide-books that rebutted those who found fault with the climate and city. Most callous was the brochure produced by the Business Men's Club of San Antonio for distribution on the nation's railroads. It assured travelers that those who died of consumption were to blame: they "unfortunately put off coming to this healthy climate until it [was] too late for them to be benefited." This breathless claim was not as confident as it appeared. An attendant graph of the city's mortality rate—14.95 deaths per 1,000—contained this important caveat: "based on residents only." The defenders of the sick-tourist trade knew, but were unwilling to publicly acknowledge, the high incidence of death associated with tuberculosis; they knew but refused to admit the potential threat this disease posed to the community's health.

To open up a debate on the link between a lucrative business that depended on communal ignorance, Dr. Frank Paschal and other local doctors publicized the relevant health statistics. The numbers were unsettling. Of the 775 deaths in San Antonio in 1886, 154 were attributed to pulmonary tuberculosis; in 1890, 40 percent of all deaths were caused by TB. These alarmingly high numbers were a direct result of the city's long-standing campaign to encourage consumptives to come to South Texas. In 1894–95, 220 of the 325 individuals who died of tuberculosis had lived in San Antonio less than a year. From these visitors the city was reaping a cruel harvest.

More deadly still was its failure to accept that the disease was contagious. When medical professionals urged the city council to enact antispitting ordinances and to regulate the spas and boardinghouses that housed the terminally ill, they were ignored. When, in concert with state medical officials, they pressed the legislature to quarantine Texas against "non-resident consumptives," they were attacked for undercutting the local economy. Not until the 1920s were they able to convince the community that the costs of tending the victims of "white plague" far outstripped the financial benefits to be wrung from their misery.

Depending on the illness of strangers, and drawing off the trailing of cattle, sustained San Antonio's economy through the first decade of the twentieth century. But several factors fundamentally altered the terrain on which future tourism could be built: the medical assault on marketing the city as a health haven, and the prohibitionist impulse that outlawed gambling in Texas in 1907 and alcohol a decade later. Eventually, a shift in economic orientation reinforced the role tourism played in moving San Antonio from its preindustrial origins to a postindustrial service center—all without the brutal messiness of industrialization. This transition offered distinct advantages for the construction of venues for visitors and closed off possibilities for a richer, more substantial local economy. Twentieth-century tourism, like its nineteenth-century predecessor, was simultaneously a boon and a bust.

One of those who recognized this tension and proposed a resolution for it was Thomas W. Pierce, president of the Galveston, Harrisburg, and San Antonio Railroad. While the citizens celebrated the line's arrival in 1877, Pierce worried that the iron horse would trample the city's "ancient quaintness." He hoped growth could be confined to the undeveloped edges in a spatial segregation that would reinforce the city's antiquated charm and exotic landscape. San Antonio's ruins were too valuable to turn into rubble.

Yet rubble they became. Around the GH&SA station grew a bustling district of warehouses, hostelries, and transportation services; six years later this pattern of development was replicated when the International and Great Northern Railroad laid down its tracks immediately west of Cattlemen's Square. To facilitate traffic between these new economic nodes, the once-narrow, twisted streets were widened and straightened, obliterating the architecture that had caught Pierce's eye. Mule-powered trolley cars clattered through this more geometric streetscape, and the effect, newspaper editor James P. Newcomb observed, was "like the intrusion of a flashily dressed, vulgar stranger upon the society of a genteel, old fashioned citizen."

Others worried that the reconstruction of the city's central core threatened landmarks like the Alamo. A group of preservationists lobbied the state to purchase a portion of the fabled battleground, including the chapel; it did so in 1883, and this purchase, when combined with later acquisitions in the early twentieth century, rounded out the site. These actions established an important connection between the denotation of this "historic" space and tourism: hallowing the ground on which so much blood had been spilled created a shrine to which any number of good patriots would journey. But they would only flock to San Antonio if the shrine's heralded past was protected. Should monuments continue to fall to "the storm of progress," the *Express* editorialized in 1912, should the citizenry continue to "be careless custodians of the goose that lays our golden egg," there would be a substantial economic ramification. "The tourist comes because he has heard of San Antonio's fame as a picturesque, historically interesting city. He brings millions of dollars annually." History sells.

Yet asking who it was being sold to, and why, reveals the degree to which the reorganization of Alamo Plaza reflected changes in the contemporary social order. In the 1840s, when the U.S. Army leased the Alamo chapel as a supply depot, its presence stimulated commerce to such an extent that the plaza began to supplant the once dominant Main and Military Plazas. The railroad's arrival generated additional hotels, boardinghouses, and stores, which were filled with the increasing number of visitors making a pilgrimage to the Alamo.

What they came to venerate, like the evolving sources of income that had shaped the plaza's new economy, was an Alamo that served as a marker of both a revolutionary past and a "critical symbol of modernity." Anthropologist Richard Flores notes that, by breaking from "the social content and spatial logic of the earlier [Spanish] plaza tradition" and emerging as "a source of income producing property" intrinsic to late-nineteenth-century capitalism, Alamo Plaza was ensured "a place in the present, and future, [for] a particular social order." The emerging Anglo domination of the economy, politics, and culture, bound up with the "remapping of San Antonio around the Alamo," enabled the new elite "to solidify [its] hold on the local geographic and social terrain." Through the landmark, it advanced "a particular mythological past of Anglo-American heroism and Mexican tyranny," freeing millions of subsequent visitors to bear witness to the bloody 1836 battle as yet another moment in American triumphalism.

Manifest destiny was an element in the various plans to reconceive the San Antonio River. They all depended, however, on some of the first words written about the stream. In May 1716, after a long march to the San Antonio area, Capitán Domingo Ramón wrote, "Crossing two dry creek beds we reached a water spring on level land, which we named San Pedro." The spring's flow led him to conclude with practiced eye that there was enough water in the locality to sustain urban growth. Many mid-nineteenth-century travelers acknowledged a critical relationship between San Antonio and its river. German scientist Ferdinand Roemer was charmed by the "location of the city in the broad valley, watered by the beautiful stream and surrounded by gently sloping hills," and thought it an "earthly paradise." In this semi-arid landscape, water was capital.

It was priceless in another sense. Roemer was transfixed by the river's recreational use: "It is quite a startling spectacle to see here just above the bridge in the heart of the city, a number of Mexican women and girls bathing entirely naked." Smitten by their fluid grace, Roemer continued to stare: "Several times a few of them were carried near us by the stream[;] then they would dive and reappear again quite a distance below the bridge. If this was done to hide themselves from our view, it was the wrong thing to do, for the water was so clear that one could see the smallest pebble at the bottom." A different aesthetic pleasure halted Frederick Law Olmsted in his tracks. "We irresistibly stop to examine" the river, he wrote, because "we are so struck with its beauty. It is of a rich blue and pure as crystal, flowing rapidly but noiselessly over pebbles and between reedy banks. One could lean for hours over the bridge-rail."

Capturing the river's sensual quality and meditative character has been central to twentieth-century schemes to integrate it into the tourist economy. That required—as it had with the Alamo—disconnecting it from its Spanish and Mexican heritage. As the city exploded in size in the late nineteenth century, and redoubled during the first decades of the twentieth, it swallowed up farmlands that the acequias once watered. Many were abandoned or buried as new roads were constructed over them and a modern sewage and water system bisected them. Moreover, as with most urban river systems, the San Antonio River became a disposal for garbage, litter, and effluent. Its flow was reduced further as the city drilled artesian wells to slake the growing urban thirst, often drying up the spring-fed river. The *San Antonio Express* lamented in 1911 that although few "cities possess so great a natural asset as a winding, tree-lined stream such as the San Antonio River," the river had "dwindled to a sluggish current running through neglected banks over a riverbed covered with slime and silt."

That the river was a mess, paradoxically, allowed the community to debate its future. Many of the business elite, sick of its stench and longing to profit from its disappearance, proposed that it be piped underground with streets platted along its former course, generating a rush of street-level trade; for them, the river as a river had no current value, and thus it could be obliterated. For others, its potential far outweighed its dreary state. Reformers pushed a plan to increase streamflow and dress up the river's banks. The economic payoff would come by using its newly won beauty (and a confused appropriation of local history) to lure a carefree clientele to its waters. Along this "vast park," which at night would be illuminated "by myriad lightbulbs," local Mexicans "dressed in the garb of Aztec Indians will paddle canoes, filled with tourists."

This lurid fantasy of the river as a zone of entertainment

began to take hold, accelerating the process by which this natural space would become increasingly artificial. One sign of this was a significant shift in nomenclature; in time the river would become known simply as the Riverwalk. But that evolution took the better part of the twentieth century. After the devastating 1921 flood, commercial agents redoubled their efforts to funnel the dangerous watercourse underground, an attack a number of civic organizations deflected. By 1929, this coalition sponsored a riverside design project called "The Shops of Aragon and Romula." As its name suggests, it wrapped a mundane commercial enterprise in a patina of Spanish exoticism, suggesting a romanticized landscape in which visitors would frolic and consume.

The plan was developed in the late 1930s, but the new system of pathways and staircases, designed to facilitate tourists' movement along the river's banks, was strikingly underutilized until the 1960s. Seeking to convert a large portion of the central business district into a tourist playground, the planners of HemisFair '68 recognized that the river could stitch together many of the disparate elements of a new urban fabric. That its waters could bring coherence to a site was revealed in the Hilton Corporation's investment in the construction of the Palacio del Rio Hotel. Rising up twenty-one stories on land located between the San Antonio River and a new exhibition hall, Palacio del Rio opens in two directions: its elevators and lobbies serve as a corridor for conventioneers and guests to cycle between riverside restaurants, bars, and shops, and street-level convention space.

This crucial linkage sparked a gold rush: since 1968, many hotels have attempted to replicate this connection. These anchors,

and smaller establishments located just off-river, annually introduce tens of thousands of guests to the Riverwalk, an increasing
volume of traffic that supports any number of businesses and
dramatically underscores the venue's profound economic impact.
Its profitability is one reason the river has all but disappeared.
Divorced from its original watershed, it is now a hydraulic system—complete with tunnels, pumps, and recycling systems art-
fully concealed from the casual gaze.

Not all is illusory. As early-twentieth-century activists had
hoped, the Riverwalk has become the communal artery and civic
stage, albeit without buff Aztec warriors plying languid waters. A
series of parades and processions that crowd the calendar and
embody a mix of cultural, economic, social, and religious values
makes full use of the paths and river surface. Even spontaneous
celebrations sweep down these waters: when the troops came
home in 1945, they floated through the cheers of a grateful citizenry, as did the San Antonio Spurs after their 1999 and 2003
NBA championship runs.

Yet for all its cultural significance and dramatic space, and
despite the billions of dollars it generates, the Riverwalk has not
been an unalloyed windfall. San Antonio has long been one of the
country's poorest large cities. Yet its poverty comes conjoined with
a remarkably low level of unemployment. What accounts for this
anomaly? A 1999 study underwritten by the San Antonio Area
Tourism Council concluded that tourism was responsible directly
and indirectly for the creation of more than 78,000 jobs (approximately 12 percent of the workforce), and for the generation of
nearly $2 billion in wages. These figures reflect the industry's

robust health, concludes council president Carol O'Malley, "and we need to make sure it stays that way."

The tourism industry's strength, critics retort, is predicated on the continued immiseration of its workers. That is why in the mid-1990s an ad hoc coalition of grassroots activists and labor organizers began to attack the city's use of tax abatements to subsidize the construction of downtown hotels. The issue helped topple Mayor Thornton in 1997 and in 2000 troubled his successor's final year in office. In the 1997 campaign, City Councilman Howard Peak had used tax abatements as a wedge issue to oust Thornton from office, and a year later he helped pass legislation calling for their use only if the corporations receiving them provided a substantial number of "living wage" jobs. But in the spring of 2000, when he asked that an exception be made for the same 1,200-room Sheraton Hotel project that had derailed his predecessor's political ambitions, the mayor's argument sparked a furor. On March 23, some 600 demonstrators packed council chambers and, after two hours of blistering testimony, the politicians delayed consideration of the Sheraton tax abatement proposal. Although the protesters congratulated themselves for winning a temporary reprieve, theirs was a Pyrrhic victory. As with the mayor, they refused to question the dominant place of tourism in the city's economy and the dangerous dependency this situation has produced. Another arch-foe of the tax abatement project, *Express-News* columnist Carlos Guerra, wrote, "San Antonians don't dislike tourists, the tourist industry or the thousands of jobs it provides." That has always been the trap.

Holy Grail

Visions of a gilded future entranced San Antonians in the fall of 2002. News that the city was in the hunt to land an $800 million Toyota plant sparked a gold rush of speculations about its potential boost to a sagging economy (state tax revenues alone were estimated at $20 million); its presumed impact on a tepid job market (more than 2,000 workers annually would construct some 150,000 Toyota Tundra trucks); and its projected cultural reverberations. Many felt that this proposed facility, in combination with its many suppliers, would single-handedly rewrite the city's economic history, introducing industrial work to a post–World War Two service economy. Were San Antonio to beat its competitors, it would find itself on uncharted terrain: to go forward, we would have to go back in time.

The metaphorical U-turn became official in February 2003 when Fujio Cho, CEO of Toyota Motor Corporation, flew into town to headline a raucous celebration. A well-heeled and well-connected throng of 1,000 jammed into the balloon-filled

Institute of Texan Cultures, located along the downtown stretch
of McAllister Freeway. The institute is a remarkably unattractive
structure, its bunkerlike form set within a moat and surrounded
by large berms. Its dour facade did not dampen the elation of
those who pushed inside, however. Smiling broadly, the governor
and lieutenant governor of Texas, members of the city's congressional delegation, and a host of local and state power brokers
cheered, whistled, and stomped as speaker after speaker extolled
the city's incentive plan (which totaled roughly $130 million) and
the state's largesse (it chipped in $15 million to build a new rail
line to the plant, among other goodies). But the loudest roar was
reserved for the new day that CEO Cho promised the community. "Besides being a great place to live and work, San Antonio is
a city of the future," he said, at which point he was interrupted by
a thunderous ovation. The city's geographical location, which
once had retarded its economic development, was now heralded as
an asset. South Texas, Cho said, lay smack in the middle of an
important corridor for North American trade that "will undoubt-
edly serve as a vital link tomorrow for business all over the world."

We have heard such grand claims before. Indeed, thirty-five
years earlier, civic leaders were convinced that the site where the
Toyota extravaganza occurred would also spark an economic miracle for the benighted region. HemisFair '68, a mini–World's
Fair, would be San Antonio's bid for greater international promi-
nence; its promoters argued that the city was slated for great
things because it stood at the "Confluence of Civilizations of the
Americas." All told, thirty nations—including Japan—set up
shop in HemisFair Park for the six-month run. The fair opened

April 6, 1968, two days after Martin Luther King Jr.'s assassination. More than six million visitors toured the ninety-two-acre site filled with national and state pavilions (Texas's facility would be converted into the Institute of Texan Cultures), art and cultural exhibits, and the usual midway fare (mock western shootouts and a bare-breasted Indian maiden). For all its glitz and glamour, the event was a financial disaster. When it closed in October, HemisFair '68 had lost an estimated $17 million.

Despite the glaring deficit, the exposition had a sustained impact on the city's central core. HemisFair prompted the construction of the first new downtown hotels since the early twentieth century, and the siting of the Palacio del Rio and La Mansion del Rio hotels on the Riverwalk paved the way for subsequent development along its landscaped paths. Local investors also launched what would grow into the La Quinta motel chain. New restaurants flourished, too, some of which have survived to feed a swelling number of conventioneers who have made good use of the ever-expanding convention center—itself located on the Riverwalk, and with its antecedents in former fair exhibition space. With HemisFair '68, tourism fully came of age.

The event's social significance was much less profound. Although many of its planners had been integral to the voluntary desegregation of the city's restaurants in the early 1960s, their efforts, the NAACP charged at the time, were not enough. In general, African Americans worried that the fair would deflect the city's attention from resolving enduring inequities. Some of the more obvious forms of discrimination disappeared by the end of the 1960s, including segregation of parks, schools, restaurants, and public transportation. African Americans have also secured a seat at the political table: ever since the mid-1970s, when a federal lawsuit forced a charter reform that required the creation of districts represented by councilmen and women, District 2, which contains the historic black east side neighborhoods, has always had an African American representative.

For all these successes and more, inequalities remain. East side schools tend to underperform, work opportunities are scarce, and the built landscape suffers from considerable neglect. Even the community's political clout, as measured by its long-standing representation on city council, may not last; by the late twentieth century, Latinos made up a majority of District 2's population. This situation has troubled the Rev. Claude Black, a legendary east side African American community leader and a former member of city council. Convinced that the postfair "wave of prosperity has never been felt by the majority of black people," he concluded in the spring of 2003 that the east side was "in worse shape than it was 35 years ago."

Yet even if the "idea of HemisFair putting us on the map is kind of overblown," in the words of local historian T. R. Fehrenbach, it triggered an intangible, but very real, alteration in the communal mindset. HemisFair, Fehrenbach said, laid "the groundwork for San Antonio to modernize." He has a point. In the decades before the fair, virtually every attempt to industrialize the regional economy had encountered sharp opposition from the power elite. In the 1910s and 1920s, some clever entrepreneurs proposed taking advantage of the U.S. Army's substantial assets in town (it then had three major bases, two of them airfields) by establishing an airplane manufacturing plant; the proposal gained no traction with the local Chamber of Commerce and was never pursued. A Ford Motor Company plant in the 1930s reportedly became a cropper of the same intransigence, as would an early 1940s offer from the federal government to underwrite the construction of an army aircraft manufacturing facility. Fearful that industrialization would lead to unionized labor and escalating wages, and unleash a social revolution they could not control, the Chamber of Commerce, elite entrepreneurs, and politicians spurned opportunities to diversify and strengthen the city's commercial prospects.

That's no longer the case. Look "what happened when Toyota said they might come here," Fehrenbach told the *Express-News*. "Every civic and political leader is delirious. That sums up the huge changes in San Antonio." Perhaps that's why the organizers of the February 2003 Toyota celebration picked the Institute of Texan Cultures to host the mega–welcoming party. There was no better place from which to signal to the community that the city was poised to enter a new stage in its economic development, a stage that marked a significant break from the tourist economy HemisFair '68 had done so much to foster.

As the fair's rocky finances would suggest and the complexities of its legacy would indicate, however, predicting San Antonio's future is a tricky thing. Indeed, no sooner had the confetti been swept up from the institute's floor and the balloons pulled from the ceiling than a wave of bad economic news rolled in. The city's small semiconductor industry was closing down; more than 1,100 workers, many of whom earned up to $70,000 a year, were laid off at the Philips and Sony plants. Like other communities around the world in the mid-1980s, San Antonio had pursued this industry in quest of economic diversification and income generation. Through a blueprint for growth known as Target '90, Mayor Henry Cisneros had focused on luring high-tech jobs in silicon chip manufacturing to South Texas, with hopes of capitalizing on, if not replicating, nearby Austin's phenomenal investment in computer research and development. When VSLI (later Philips) set up a 330,000-square-foot plant in 1988, followed two years later by Sony's 550,000-square-foot site, it appeared that Cisneros's dreams were coming to fruition. Until, that is, the computer industry went into a free fall in the late 1990s and chip orders plummeted, shuttering plants everywhere. This was not the first time San Antonio (and its urban peers) had discovered that global market corrections can have deep and dire local consequences. Nor, I imagine, will it be the last.

Index

CHAR MILLER is professor of history and director of the urban studies program at Trinity University. His books include the award-winning *Gifford Pinchot and the Making of Modern Environmentalism* and *The Greatest Good: 100 Years of Forestry in America;* he is editor most recently of *The Atlas of Canadian and U.S. Environmental History, On the Border: An Environmental History of San Antonio,* and *Fluid Arguments: Five Centuries of Western Water Conflict.* A senior fellow at the Pinchot Institute for Conservation and a contributing writer to the *Texas Observer,* Miller lives with his wife in San Antonio.